KU-444-825

THE UPPER ROOM

WHERE THE WORLD MEETS TO PRAY

Daniele Och
UK editor

INVITATIONAL
INTERDENOMINATIONAL
INTERNATIONAL

37 LANGUAGES
Multiple formats are available in some languages

The Bible Reading Fellowship
15 The Chambers, Vineyard
Abingdon OX14 3FE
brf.org.uk

The Bible Reading Fellowship (BRF) is a Registered Charity (233280)

ISBN 978 1 80039 031 7

Originally published in the USA by The Upper Room® **upperroom.org**
US edition © 2021 The Upper Room, Nashville, TN (USA). All rights reserved.
This edition © The Bible Reading Fellowship 2021
Cover image © iStock.com/Graphixel

Acknowledgements

Scripture quotations marked with the following abbreviations are taken from the
version shown. Where no acronym is given, the quotation is taken from the same
version as the headline reference.

NIV: The Holy Bible, New International Version (Anglicised edition) copyright © 1979,
1984, 2011 by Biblica. Used by permission of Hodder & Stoughton Publishers, an
Hachette UK company. All rights reserved. 'NIV' is a registered trademark of Biblica.
UK trademark number 1448790.

NRSV: The New Revised Standard Version of the Bible, Anglicised Edition, copyright
© 1989, 1995 by the Division of Christian Education of the National Council of the
Churches of Christ in the USA. Used by permission. All rights reserved.

CEB: copyright © 2011 by Common English Bible.

KJV: the Authorised Version of the Bible (The King James Bible), the rights in which
are vested in the Crown, are reproduced by permission of the Crown's Patentee,
Cambridge University Press.

A catalogue record for this book is available from the British Library

Printed by Gutenberg Press, Tarxien, Malta

How to use *The Upper Room*

The Upper Room is ideal in helping us spend a quiet time with God each day. Each daily entry is based on a passage of scripture and is followed by a meditation and prayer. Each person who contributes a meditation to the magazine seeks to relate their experience of God in a way that will help those who use *The Upper Room* every day.

Here are some guidelines to help you make best use of *The Upper Room*:

1 Read the passage of scripture. It is a good idea to read it more than once, in order to have a fuller understanding of what it is about and what you can learn from it.
2 Read the meditation. How does it relate to your own experience? Can you identify with what the writer has outlined from their own experience or understanding?
3 Pray the written prayer. Think about how you can use it to relate to people you know or situations that need your prayers today.
4 Think about the contributor who has written the meditation. Some users of the *The Upper Room* include this person in their prayers for the day.
5 Meditate on the 'Thought for the day' and the 'Prayer focus', perhaps using them again as the focus for prayer or direction for action.

Why is it important to have a daily quiet time? Many people will agree that it is the best way of keeping in touch every day with the God who sustains us and who sends us out to do his will and show his love to the people we encounter each day. Meeting with God in this way reassures us of his presence with us, helps us to discern his will for us and makes us part of his worldwide family of Christian people through our prayers.

I hope that you will be encouraged as you use the magazine regularly as part of your daily devotions, and that God will richly bless you as you read his word and seek to learn more about him.

Daniele Och
UK editor

BRF needs you!

If you're one of our thousands of regular *Upper Room* readers, you will know all about the impact that regular Bible reading has on your faith and the value of daily notes to encourage and inspire you. *Upper Room* readers share those blessings with Christians across the world; they know that every day, in each part of the day, someone, somewhere is reading the same meditation.

If you enjoy reading *The Upper Room*, and love the feeling of being part of a worldwide family, would you be willing to share your experience with others? Could you ask for a brief slot during church notices or write a short piece for your church magazine or website? Do you belong to groups, formal or informal, where you could share your experience of using Bible reading notes and encourage others to try them?

It doesn't need to be complicated or nerve-wracking: just answering these three questions in what you say or write will get your message across:

1 How do Bible reading notes help you grow in your faith?
2 Where, when and how do you use them?
3 What would you say to people who don't already use them?

We can supply further information if you need it and would love to hear about it if you do give a talk or write an article.

For more information:

- Email **enquiries@brf.org.uk**
- Telephone BRF on **+44 (0)1865 319700** Mon–Fri 9.30–17.00
- Write to us at BRF, 15 The Chambers, Vineyard, Abingdon OX14 3FE

Always worthwhile

'The Advocate, the Holy Spirit, whom the Father will send in my name, will teach you all things and will remind you of everything I have said to you.'
John 14:26 (NIV)

As a mother, wife and full-time editor, I nearly always feel as if I have too much to do and not enough time or energy to do all of it as well as I would like. Nearly everyone I know feels this way at some time or another. In facing daily challenges and especially in facing the injustice and suffering in the world, perhaps it is human nature to wonder: What if I can't give enough? What if the best I can do is not good enough? Should I even try? The writers in this issue share stories of faithful courage and perseverance that offer a resounding and encouraging response: Yes! Efforts toward love and justice – even seemingly insignificant ones – are always worthwhile.

On the Day of Pentecost, God sent the Holy Spirit to dwell among us so that we would never have to depend solely on our own strength. Even when we think that what we can do or give is not enough, it is still worth doing what is right, giving what we have, and being who we are for the good of the world. The Holy Spirit – our advocate and comforter – rekindles the message of Christ in our hearts and sends us out into the world to love our neighbours.

Thankfully, God does not ask for perfection, only our faithful participation. Our loving God continually calls us back to rest and renewal, then sends us out with the strength and power of the Holy Spirit to love and serve God's world once again.

Lindsay L. Gray
Editorial Director, The Upper Room

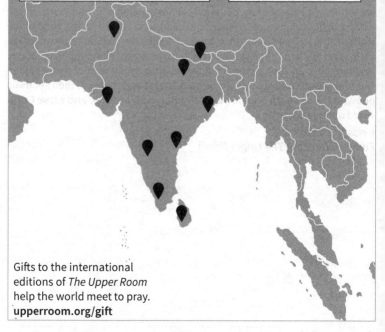

Gujarati
It is a goal of the Gujarati edition team to develop a mobile application to make the devotional guide more accessible and to expand distribution.

Odia
The publishing team of *Dhyana Kothari*, the Odia edition of *The Upper Room*, is partnering with local campus ministries to share the magazine with college students.

Editions of *The Upper Room* are printed in:
- India – English, Gujarati, Hindi, Kannada, Malayalam, Odia and Telugu
- Nepal
- Pakistan
- Sri Lanka – English, Sinhala and Tamil

Gifts to the international editions of *The Upper Room* help the world meet to pray.
upperroom.org/gift

The editor writes...

And whatever you do, whether in word or deed, do it all in the name of the Lord Jesus, giving thanks to God the Father through him.
Colossians 3:17 (NIV)

Over the past year, the pandemic has caused an upsurge in many people working from home. As a result, a lot of advice, along with some funny stories, has emerged on how to handle one's home life infringing on one's work space. The merging of these two areas, the professional and the domestic, was brought home to me (excuse the pun) during a recent phone call I had. The assistant at the other end of the phone apologised for the noise in the background. She explained that she was working in her kitchen and that her husband had to answer the door to take a delivery, which also set their dog barking.

I sympathised with her. Although I was by no means an important customer she needed to impress, had I been in her shoes I would have been anxious about the impinging noise of home life coming across as unprofessional. She did not, however, need to apologise. When I heard a bit of the context of her domestic life, it reminded me that this anonymous voice I was speaking with was an actual human being, not just a helpdesk assistant.

Modern life tends to get separated into different categories – work, family, hobbies, politics and so on – and so we can define ourselves and others in terms of those categories. It can also be all too easy to see God in the same way. How often do I think of God as belonging in the category of faith or religion, as distinct from my work life or family life, my hobbies or my politics?

In his letter to the Colossians, the apostle Paul writes of Jesus: 'In him all things were created… He is before all things, and in him all things hold together' (1:16–17). Jesus is not contained within or defined by the narrow categories I might try to put him in. Neither does he merely merge some of those categories together. Jesus completely transcends them. He created all things, and he holds all things together.

This is good news. Jesus is not just interested in a narrow part of our lives – the things we usually think of as religious or spiritual or faith-based. *Whatever* we do, we are to do it in his name. In doing so, we find that to follow Jesus is not about becoming a more religious or spiritual or holy person per se. It is to become the fully alive, actual human being he made us to be.

Daniele Och
UK editor

Kind words

Read Luke 6:20–31

'Do to others as you would have them do to you.'
Luke 6:31 (NIV)

My apartment is close to a large shopping centre, and I often visit the supermarket there. Even though there are many checkout counters at the exit of the supermarket, I usually push my shopping trolley to one familiar cashier who has always been very friendly and efficient.

One day she looked tired and sad, which was unusual. I wanted to cheer her up, so I told her how much I like her friendly attitude in serving customers. She looked at me and her eyes were filled with tears. She said, 'Thank you for your kind words. My husband died yesterday in the hospital, and you have consoled me.'

I believe that God's Spirit prompted me to start that conversation. How often do we notice the needs of our neighbours? How often do we respond to God's prompting to speak a word of kindness? If we are willing to listen, we may hear God's voice guiding us to speak a word that someone needs to hear.

Prayer: *Loving God, help us to listen for your prompting, and help us to speak words of kindness and peace to those around us. Amen*

Thought for the day: Today I will look for an opportunity to speak God's peace to someone.

Maire Simm (Tallinn, Estonia)

'Why, God?'

Read Judges 6:11–20

'Pardon me, my lord,' Gideon replied, 'but if the Lord is with us, why has all this happened to us?'

Judges 6:13 (NIV)

As I write, the Covid-19 quarantine is in place, and my husband, who is in a skilled nursing facility, is close to death. Thankfully, I was allowed in to see him one last time. Needless to say, life seems very difficult right now. Further, once he passes on, I know it will be too risky to even consider having friends and family gather to comfort and support me. I will be alone – and yet not alone. God is with me, though I must admit I occasionally share Gideon's sentiments. When I came upon that scripture during my daily quiet time, I laughed out loud.

I suspect I'm not the only believer who has asked this question in times of trial. Reassuringly, God didn't condemn Gideon but continually worked with him, increasing and building Gideon's faith. Gideon, to his credit, also went forward trusting God despite his doubts, and thereby triumphed.

In times of doubt, we can feel free to be honest with God, knowing God understands. However, we can also bravely follow where God leads, trusting in spite of our fears.

Prayer: *Dear Father, sustain us when we question you and have doubts about situations we do not understand. Give us the faith and courage to follow you anyway. Amen*

Thought for the day: God understands my frailty and my fears.

Sandra Still (North Carolina, USA)

PRAYER FOCUS: FAMILIES UNABLE TO GATHER IN TIMES OF GRIEF

The scary balloon

Read Isaiah 43:1–7

'Do not fear, for I am with you.'
Isaiah 43:5 (NRSV)

One day I was in the kitchen when suddenly I heard my young dog barking in another room. When I went to see what was going on, I found him staring at a 'happy birthday' balloon attached to a vase of flowers on a table. The balloon was moving only slightly but enough to distress him. Something that I knew to be quite harmless had created much anxiety in him.

So it often is with situations that we do not fully understand. When I was a teenager, my father's heart attack loomed before me, filling me with the fear that he might die. Many years later my own heart attack filled me with similar apprehension about the future. Was I going to live? Would I be able to continue to work? What about my family?

I found great reassurance in my faith and in God's word and presence. In today's scripture, a message of comfort and reassurance comes to the beleaguered Jewish exiles in Babylon. God assured them that he was with them still and working out all things for their ultimate good.

It is good to know that whatever our fearful situations – illness, loss of a job, financial struggles – all are opportunities to remember God's love for us and to receive God's grace and courage to move forward in faith.

Prayer: *Help us, heavenly Father, to release fear and reclaim faith in the face of trouble, trusting that you will see us through. Amen*

Thought for the day: God's presence helps us live with peace and confidence.

J. Leland Collins (Virginia, USA)

Spiritual connection

Read 2 Peter 1:3–8

Rejoice always, pray continually, give thanks in all circumstances; for this is God's will for you in Christ Jesus.
1 Thessalonians 5:16–18 (NIV)

The older I get, the more I try to maintain a healthy body by eating well and getting regular physical exercise. However, there are days when grabbing a fast-food meal is more appetising and easier than cooking a healthy meal at home, and the thought of sitting on my sofa catching up on one of my favourite shows is more appealing than changing my clothes and driving to the path where I take my 40-minute after-dinner walk. I know that in the long run I will feel better and be happier with myself if I put in the extra effort, but it takes discipline to get those rewards.

The same can be said about my spiritual health. It takes discipline to make the extra effort to maintain a close relationship with God. There are so many distractions in our world today, and sometimes it takes diligence to turn away from things like checking emails and social media and to settle into prayer and Bible reading. Today's quoted scripture reminds us that God wants us to rejoice, pray and give thanks. If we make the effort to set aside time to do this daily, our reward can be a healthy spiritual connection with God.

Prayer: *Dear Lord, help us to quiet the distractions so that we can spend precious time with you. Amen*

Thought for the day: I can improve my spiritual health by reading God's word and praying daily.

Linda L. White (Illinois, USA)

Always ready

Read Acts 17:16–34

Preach the word; be prepared in season and out of season; correct, rebuke and encourage – with great patience and careful instruction.
2 Timothy 4:2 (NIV)

My mother was not a Christian, and I never tried to force my faith on her when we talked. Then one day my mother said she wanted to go to church and know the Jesus that I know.

I have similar experiences with some of the sellers in the traditional market where I like to shop. I do not criticise those who have different beliefs. I praise those who are diligent in worship, and I do not hesitate to express my faith.

One day a seller in the market was curious about what makes me so joyful, so I told her about Jesus – the source of my joy. She did not immediately accept Jesus, but after several years she told me that she wanted to know Jesus and be joyful too.

This seller reminds me of Damaris and Dionysius from today's reading, who believed Paul's teaching about Jesus even though others did not. In today's quoted scripture, Paul encouraged Timothy to preach and to be prepared both in and out of season. Whether others believe in Jesus is the work of God. But we can learn from Paul to express our faith to others anywhere and at any time.

Prayer: *Dear Lord, let our lives be to your glory. Help us to share the joy of your word with others. Amen*

Thought for the day: I can share the love of Jesus at any time.

Linda Chandra (Banten, Indonesia)

Free from anxiety

Read Psalm 121

Do not be anxious about anything, but in every situation, by prayer and petition, with thanksgiving, present your requests to God.
Philippians 4:6 (NIV)

When I was in middle school, I went through a three-year period when I was injured several times. While playing basketball, I suffered a concussion, broke my wrist and sprained my ankle. Every time I healed, I got hurt again. I became anxious even stepping on to the court, because I was scared something bad was going to happen.

Finally I decided to ask God for help, and God renewed my strength and courage. I also realised how much I had gained from my experiences. Not being able to play for long periods of time helped me to see how much I loved basketball. I also learned how to play the game more safely, which will allow me to be active for a long time to come.

Our struggles and the anxiety they can cause are part of life, but we don't have to go through them alone. When we pray and trust God for help, God will see us through our toughest situations. Most of the time after what I am worrying about has passed, I realise that I don't need to worry because God is looking out for me all the time.

Prayer: *O God, bring peace to all who are suffering and courage to all who are afraid. Amen*

Thought for the day: In times of anxiety, I will look to God for guidance and comfort.

Adam Pitman (North Carolina, USA)

True wealth

Read 1 Peter 4:8–11

God loves a cheerful giver.
2 Corinthians 9:7 (CEB)

It always gives my heart a lift in the morning to put out some crumbs for the squirrels and birds in the yard outside my apartment. I enjoy watching them come and busily feast on their find. Although I know it's our heavenly Father who ultimately provides for all creatures (see Matthew 6:26), I love that I get to be an instrument in that process.

I love the fact that God's care can flow through me to those in need. But I don't have much money, and I often feel frustrated that I can't do more. Yet I give whatever I can and feel blessed to be able to do so.

Then I remind myself that true wealth is having something – anything – to give away. Such wealth means sharing something of myself. It means being able to alleviate suffering or just enrich another's life. In addition to whatever financial resources I have, my spirit rejoices when I can offer a kind word, a listening ear, a home-cooked meal, godly advice, an encouraging smile, a thoughtful gesture or simply my time.

Even if all I have to give are crumbs, I am indeed rich when I give to others with love.

Prayer: *Dear Father, help us always to give cheerfully, as you so faithfully give to us. In Christ's name we ask this. Amen*

Thought for the day: My smallest gift can be a huge blessing.

Victoria Walsh (Montana, USA)

PRAYER FOCUS: THOSE WHO DO NOT FEEL EQUIPPED TO DO GOD'S WORK

By God's grace

Read Ephesians 2:1–10

It is by grace you have been saved.

Ephesians 2:5 (NIV)

Two years ago I visited a well-known pottery factory in Northern Ireland. The pottery made there – vases, figurines, bowls and dinnerware – is crafted to very high standards. I took advantage of my visit to join a group being guided through the production process.

The final stage – quality control – especially drew my attention. Each item was individually inspected. If an article was found to be blemished in any way, it was smashed into pieces and discarded. Many of the items set aside for destruction had faults so minor I had trouble finding them.

As I watched the destruction of the imperfect pieces, I thought how crucially significant it is that God does not treat us that way. Ephesians 2:5 says, 'It is by grace you have been saved.' By the grace of God, our salvation does not depend on what we have done, but on God's grace through Christ – who Christ is and what he has done for us at the cross.

We don't deserve salvation, and we cannot earn it; but God gives it to us anyway. So when we respond to God's call, God will never reject us.

Prayer: *Loving God, help us to remember that it is only by your grace that we receive your salvation. We are grateful for the assurance and joy it brings. In Jesus' name. Amen*

Thought for the day: God does not discard me; God redeems me.

Awlwyn Balnave (British Columbia, Canada)

Living word

Read 2 Peter 1:12–19

All who are led by the Spirit of God are children of God.
Romans 8:14 (NRSV)

Every morning before school and work, our family spends time together reading from *The Upper Room*. We have done this since our son, now ten years old, started kindergarten. It gives us a positive way to start our day, and it helps us turn our focus towards Jesus.

We use the online edition of *The Upper Room*, so there have been a few times when we have experienced a glitch where our screen displays only part of the day's devotional. When this occurs, my son and I will guess the rest of that day's message and what happened to the writer. My son generally paints an uplifting picture of how he believes Jesus had a positive effect on the writer's life.

As Christians we have clues to help us interpret God's messages for us. The Bible is our compass, explaining God's gift of eternal life and salvation. And our church family, Bible study groups and fellow believers are key witnesses to God's grace.

As a parent and as a Christian, it is my duty to make sure that God's message is not merely a story or words on paper, by reflecting my faith through my actions. While each day has its challenges, the Holy Spirit has guided our family to become more like Jesus – obeying, forgiving and loving together.

Prayer: *Dear Lord, guide us to use your living word as a testimony for others who are coming to know Christ. Amen*

Thought for the day: I can help make God's word come alive for others.

Melissa Yamaguchi (Hawaii, USA)

PRAYER FOCUS: THOSE TEACHING CHILDREN ABOUT GOD

Following God's call

Read Exodus 4:10–17
Trust in the Lord with all your heart, and do not rely on your own insight.
Proverbs 3:5 (NRSV)

Years ago, in responding to God's call to pastoral ministry, I had a choice: I could continue working at my full-time job and serve as a part-time pastor, or I could give up my job and be a full-time pastor. Both are valid ways to serve God. I felt a pull towards full-time ministry, but I was uncertain if I could support my family on a pastor's salary. I kept anxiously trying to calculate my expenses against that income, and it did not look promising. I trusted that if it was God's call, it would work out, but still I was uncertain. Finally I said, 'Okay, God, if you open the door to a full-time church position, I will walk through that door.' Then I felt peace and certainty about God's call.

When we are trying to arrange life on our own terms, we cannot be fully attentive to God's call, whatever that may be. I have served as a full-time pastor for more than 25 years now and have never regretted that decision. If we begin to entrust the future to God, we can find peace and clarity.

Prayer: *Gracious and loving God, help us to truly listen and respond to your call for our lives. Help us always to trust you. Amen*

Thought for the day: God's call for me can become clearer when I trust God to provide.

Gene Lankford (Alabama, USA)

In the storm

Read Mark 4:35–41

He woke up and rebuked the wind, and said to the sea, 'Peace! Be still!' Then the wind ceased, and there was a dead calm.
Mark 4:39 (NRSV)

Due to a decline in my health, I was forced to give up my career as a primary school teacher. The job had enabled me to support my husband and myself while he finished his university degree. This time of financial difficulty has been debilitating for us. God is good and has provided us with the means to pay our rent and other bills and to buy food through government benefits. However, we have no money left over for other necessities.

As I'm writing this, my benefits will be cut in two months. I wonder how we will pay rent and cover our needs. My husband started a new job, but we're just scraping by. I try to focus on Jesus' calming presence, but the threat of homelessness strikes constant fear in me.

This afternoon I was in the kitchen when the sky suddenly turned dark. A storm blew in with strong wind and hail. Then, as quickly as it came, the squall ceased and the sun came out. As I stood on the balcony and soaked in the sunlight, my faith was renewed as I realised that my husband and I are not going through this trial alone. God is with us in the storm, caring for and protecting us. And in time, God will bring us to the other side of the storm where the sun will shine again.

Prayer: *Loving Father, thank you for your presence during our trials. When we face troubles, help us always to find you amid the storm. Amen*

Thought for the day: Even when I face troubles, God will not forsake me.

Madeline Twooney (North Rhine-Westphalia, Germany)

Listen and act

Read Isaiah 20:1–6

At that time the Lord spoke through Isaiah son of Amoz.
Isaiah 20:2 (NIV)

In today's reading, God tells the prophet Isaiah to remove his clothes and his sandals and walk around naked for three years. It was a drastic and visual message to Israel of the shame they would experience if they didn't listen to God's direction. Isaiah listened to God and took action.

While usually not as dramatic, the Lord continues to speak today, and when I hear God's call I try to take action. Early in the morning as I begin my workday, I often take a few moments to think about my friends and colleagues, asking myself, 'Do I need to reach out to someone today with a phone call or an email?' God's still small voice often brings to my mind neighbours, co-workers or relatives. Sometimes the person is surprising – someone I have not connected with in months.

I make a list of the people who come to mind and reach out to them during the day. I write a short email to some people. I call others and speak with them for a few minutes or leave them a personal message. Often when I speak with someone, they will tell me, 'I was just thinking about you today. I'm so glad you called.' When this happens I smile and am assured that I am following the directions of a loving God.

Prayer: *Loving God, help me to listen to your still, small voice and to obey your leading. Amen*

Thought for the day: Today I will listen for and obey God's guidance.

W. Terry Whalin (Colorado, USA)

The fragrance of love

Read 2 Corinthians 2:14–17
Thanks be to God, who in Christ always leads us in triumphal procession, and through us spreads in every place the fragrance that comes from knowing him.
2 Corinthians 2:14 (NRSV)

'Raise your hand when you can smell it,' I told my science students at the beginning of an activity to help them experience the concept of diffusion. I stood at the front of the classroom and sprayed floral-scented air freshener into the air. Hands of the students at the nearest lab table shot up immediately. Then, by watching the pattern of raised hands, we were able to see how the scent diffused into the air from the front of the room to the back. Eventually all students indicated that they smelled the fragrance.

Today's scripture reading reminds us that we are called to be the fragrance of Christ's love for others, as 'persons sent from God and standing in his presence'.

Just as the scent of the air freshener diffused away from where I sprayed it, the aroma of God's love spreads outward each time we serve others in the name of Jesus Christ. Offering a word of encouragement, providing a listening ear or spending time with someone in need of support are just a few of the ways we can offer God's love to others and inspire them to spread that love in their corner of the world.

Today let's look for ways to be the fragrance of Christ in a world that needs to know and experience God's love!

Prayer: *O God, because we are blessed by your love, we want to share it with everyone we meet today. Strengthen us in our work for you. Amen*

Thought for the day: Opportunities to spread God's love are all around me.

Jill Allen Maisch (Maryland, USA)

Identity in Christ

Read Galatians 3:23–29

In Christ Jesus you are all children of God through faith.
Galatians 3:26 (NIV)

During a recent job interview, I was asked to draw an identity wheel – a pie chart depicting the importance I place on my social identities. After I completed the wheel, I looked at how my gender, race, socioeconomic status, education, religion, country of origin, age, family structure and physical ability shape and define who I consider myself to be. I realised how much I conduct my life according to these identities. Then I asked myself, 'Where does Christ fit in? What if I leave no space for Christ to fill?'

I don't think we need to renounce our social identities. After all, Paul didn't deny the reality of being Jew or Gentile, male or female. He simply said that we should act as God's children all the time, under all circumstances, no matter what our social identities are. We can clothe ourselves with Christ through the presence and guidance of the Holy Spirit, so that our way of living, our thoughts, our decisions and our actions demonstrate our identity as children of God.

Prayer: *Dear God, help us always to show through our actions that we are your children. Amen*

Thought for the day: How will I show my identity as a child of God today?

Luis David Arias (Bogotá, Colombia)

Mangoes for everyone

Read Psalm 107:4–9
He satisfies the thirsty and fills the hungry with good things.
Psalm 107:9 (NIV)

Every summer, the mango trees in my neighbourhood produce an abundant harvest. Any fruit that falls over a tree-owner's fence is free to the first taker. Hundreds of beautiful, sweet mangoes fall to the ground when the wind blows, and each year I harvest the fallen fruit and freeze it to last the entire year.

When our city was hit by Hurricane Irma, we lost power for several days. All the mangoes I had recently preserved were ruined. I felt devastated. When mango season came the next year, I noticed many strangers looking for mangoes. People came on bikes, in cars and on foot. I searched daily and found none. I felt defeated.

Finally, a few blocks away, I discovered two giant bags of mangoes lying by the side of the road for anyone to take. I praised God for the discovery, yet I felt a sense of guilt. I had blamed others for taking fruit that had never belonged to me, and suddenly a gift of mangoes was given to me.

That day I learned that God will provide for all God's creatures. Our hunger will be filled. Now when I collect mangoes, I leave some of the fruit at the edge of my yard as my kind neighbours have taught me to do.

Prayer: *Dear Lord, thank you for all that you provide for us. Help us remember to share this bounty with one another in your holy name. Amen*

Thought for the day: How will I share God's merciful bounty with others?

Gretchen Nelson (Florida, USA)

Our prayer

Read Matthew 6:7–13

Be transformed by the renewing of your mind. Then you will be able to test and approve what God's will is – his good, pleasing and perfect will.

Romans 12:2 (NIV)

During my prayer time each day, I close my supplications to God with Jesus' prayer: 'Thy will be done on earth, as it is in heaven.' Were this powerful prayer to be answered in our time, I believe we would have peace in our world and love would prevail over hatred. Justice would be achieved; the intrinsic worth of everyone would be fully recognised; there would be an end to all that causes conflict and division. God's creation would be cherished by all.

I believe that the power of the Lord's Prayer is that in the act of reciting it, we are called to seek and live out God's will each day, relying on the Holy Spirit for guidance. We can share God's love with our neighbours. We can work for justice in our communities and nations. We can seek to eradicate prejudice when we see it. We can help to preserve the gifts of God's creation for future generations.

I pray that our lives will ever be inspired by our Lord's prayer as we seek to live fully as God's servants, wherever the Holy Spirit leads us.

Prayer: *Dear Lord, let your prayer be on our lips and guide our actions each day. Your will be done. Amen*

Thought for the day: The Lord's Prayer is my call to action.

Donald Huffman (North Carolina, USA)

Firm belief

Read Psalm 30:1–4

To you, O Lord, I lift up my soul. O my God, in you I trust; do not let me be put to shame; do not let my enemies exult over me.
Psalm 25:1–2 (NRSV)

When my parents died, my younger brother and I lived together. Our financial situation was difficult. He drove a bus, and I was a school-teacher. Then I was diagnosed with a brain tumour in addition to the lung problems that make breathing difficult for me.

When my brother got engaged, it was my responsibility as the older sister to plan the wedding. As the wedding date was set, I knelt down and prayed, 'O my Lord, help us to fulfil all the necessary arrangements for the wedding.'

God answered my prayer. Our friends and family offered their help and support. By the grace of God, all the wedding preparations went smoothly without any hindrance. My heart was filled with joy.

This experience strengthened my firm belief in God and in prayer. God listens to our prayers and fulfils our needs and requests when we pray with trust, faith, hope and confidence.

Prayer: *God of all comfort, help us to trust that you are with us in all situations, especially in times of trouble. As Jesus taught us, we pray, 'Our Father which art in heaven, Hallowed be thy name. Thy kingdom come. Thy will be done, as in heaven, so in earth. Give us day by day our daily bread. And forgive us our sins; for we also forgive every one that is indebted to us. And lead us not into temptation; but deliver us from evil.'* Amen*

Thought for the day: God will help me and never leave me alone.

Kausar Amen (Punjab, Pakistan)

Hope of renewal

Read Isaiah 40:27–31

Those who wait for the Lord shall renew their strength, they shall mount up with wings like eagles, they shall run and not be weary, they shall walk and not faint.

Isaiah 40:31 (NRSV)

Last week I watched what seemed to be a lizard party in my backyard. Lizards were everywhere – climbing on the fence, skittering from rock to rock, dodging behind flowers, perching on leaves and gliding across chairs and concrete. They seemed so full of joy and life that I wondered if they knew that most of them were missing their tails. When I told my nine-year-old son the missing-tail saga, he told me not to worry. He said, 'Lizards are amazing! They grow new tails!'

We may lose parts of ourselves – to chronic illness, grief, job loss, conflict or some other event. Ironically, we may seem to lose all we want to keep and gain only new sorrow. We may even lose hope.

In all our loss, it is easy to think we will never be renewed or made whole. It's easy to think we will never find joy again, that we will never laugh or see the beauty in the world. However, today's verse tells us the Lord's promise: those who trust in God will renew their strength.

We may never regain exactly what we have lost, but we can find joy in the certainty that God is with us and will renew us day by day.

Prayer: *Dear God, remind us of your promise of renewed life. Help us to live each day with joy and hope in you. Amen*

Thought for the day: With God's help, I can live in joy every day.

Kadine Christie (Alabama, USA)

PRAYER FOCUS: SOMEONE WHO HAS BEEN IN AN ACCIDENT

Treasured words

Read Psalm 119:129–136

The unfolding of your words gives light; it gives understanding to the simple.

Psalm 119:130 (NIV)

Granddad was a quiet man. But in the evenings when he settled on the sofa, poetry flowed from him. I loved to lean against his chest, my cheek on his worn, flannel shirt, and listen to the rumble and rhythm of the words as he spoke. He often recited Henry Wadsworth Longfellow's poem about the village blacksmith under the spreading chestnut tree. Knowing just when to pause or raise his voice, he transported me to another time and place. I was spellbound.

Granddad taught me that we learn from words when we treasure them. The verse from Psalm 119 above invites us to do the same with the words of God. As the source of all knowledge, God has much to teach us through the Bible. But the psalmist tells us that we'll miss the lesson if we skim over the words; rather, they're meant to be unfolded. Layer by layer, word by word, we open the divine gift. We read God's words until they're stamped in our memory and the light of understanding enters our hearts. Then those words can teach us wisdom, direct our steps, wrap us in comfort and peace, show us mercy and love, and bring us closer to God.

Prayer: *Thank you, God, for your word. Help us to unfold it like a treasured gift so that it fills our lives and our hearts. Amen*

Thought for the day: Today and every day, I will treasure God's word.

Cindy Tanquary Peavy (Alabama, USA)

Holy signs

Read Acts 5:12–16

The apostles performed many signs and wonders among the people.
Acts 5:12 (NIV)

God has given us many signs to show us how to know and follow our creator. If we look up into the sky at night, we can see what astronomers tell us are millions of galaxies, each with more stars than the number of grains of sand on the earth – a sign of God's greatness (see Genesis 1:16). Yet another sign is God's rainbow as a promise that never again will God flood the earth (see Genesis 7:4; 9:11–16). The clearest and most powerful sign our creator has given us is the cross, which demonstrates how much God loves us (see John 3:16).

What signs can we leave for others? Maybe we can help build a new school or orphanage, either by joining a team or financially supporting and praying for such a venture. Other signs could be the food we leave at a food bank or clothes we donate to the homeless. Maybe the best sign we can leave is the encouragement, time or prayer we invest to help point others in the direction of Christ Jesus.

Prayer: *Dear God, thank you for the signs you have given us. Most of all we thank you for your great love for us all. In the name of Jesus, who came to show us the way to you. Amen*

Thought for the day: What signs of God's goodness can I leave for others today?

William Elliott (Northern Ireland, United Kingdom)

Equally beautiful

Read 1 Corinthians 12:14–25

God has placed the parts in the body, every one of them, just as he wanted them to be.
1 Corinthians 12:18 (NIV)

A few years ago, my husband and I took a trip to the beachside city of Destin, Florida. I grew up in Colorado and had never seen the ocean up close. One morning, as I watched the sunrise and listened to the waves, I was overwhelmed. I thought, 'God is amazing!' I pondered how different the coast is from the mountains in Colorado. Then I realised: in one part of the country the ocean displays the glorious and awesome power of God and in another the mountains serve the same purpose. God also sets us each in different places – the place that will best display God's power and glory.

Sometimes I've compared my life to others thinking, 'Surely I should be further along than this. Surely I should have discovered some gift or talent in myself by now.' But when I compare my life to someone else's, I miss the beauty God wants to display through me.

We all have different purposes, and no purpose is better than another – just different. The mountains and the ocean are equally beautiful and both display God's glory. So it is with us. We each have our own beauty, gifts and talents – all meant to bring glory to God.

Prayer: *Dear God, thank you for creating our beautiful world. Help us to glorify you wherever we are. Amen*

Thought for the day: I can display God's beauty where I am today.

Jackie Johnson (Colorado, USA)

A good life

Read Revelation 21:1–5

This is the day that the Lord has made; let us rejoice and be glad in it.
Psalm 118:24 (NRSV)

On 1 May 2018, the meditation in *The Upper Room* was about a young boy who sat on the stairs putting pebbles in his mouth. His mother took the rocks out, but he resisted going to the dining room where dessert awaited. Finally, when he saw a chocolate cake on the table, he stopped screaming and his eyes widened with joy. I wonder if I might be like that boy.

I am in my 90s and have enjoyed a good life, including 40 years as a minister. My wife, Jackie, and I have been happily married more than 70 years. As we grow older, I am increasingly reluctant for our lives on earth to end. Together we rejoice in each day God gives us, and we want to stay here as long as we can.

Easter assures us that eternal life awaits us in heaven. Old Testament prophets and the book of Revelation describe it glowingly, but we are not ready yet. We want to continue enjoying each other, our loved ones, and the joys and beauties of earth. But the boy in the meditation may be a good reminder for us. Maybe all the joys and beauties of earth will pale in comparison to what awaits us in heaven.

Prayer: *Thank you, God, for our eternal life in Christ. Help us to await heaven with joy. Amen*

Thought for the day: The gifts God offers me do not end with this life.

Gus Browning (Texas, USA)

PRAYER FOCUS: GRATITUDE FOR THIS DAY

Signs of spring

Read Psalm 46

'Be still, and know that I am God; I will be exalted among the nations, I will be exalted in the earth.'
Psalm 46:10 (NIV)

As I write this, much of the world is gripped in the fear of coronavirus and the frustration of lockdown.

I venture out very early for my run and daily exercise, to enjoy the fresh air while avoiding people and the challenges of social distancing. Spring is unfolding and each day brings new marvels as the dawn chorus seems even louder among the quiet streets, and animals venture more into the less crowded city. Nature doesn't know there is a virus and the certainty of God's creation warms my heart and restores my faith and hope as each bud opens and each bird sings.

Running past many windows with pictures of rainbows, I am reminded of the covenant that God made with all that lives on earth (see Genesis 9:17) and of the fact that there is hope and light to follow even after dark times.

Such daily reminders reassure me that God is with us, that God will never leave nor forsake us and that God is our shelter and our refuge, a timely help in trouble. We do not need to be afraid.

Prayer: *Dear Lord, comfort all who mourn and are fearful with the sure knowledge of hope and faith in you. Amen*

Thought for the day: Today, I will look for signs of God's covenant faithfulness.

Judy Wagner (Scotland, United Kingdom)

A hopeful future

Read Jeremiah 29:1–13

I know the plans I have for you,' declares the Lord, 'plans to prosper you and not to harm you, plans to give you hope and a future.'
Jeremiah 29:11 (NIV)

Today's scripture came to me at a time when I felt hopeless. I was very poor, my son had committed suicide and less than a year later my grandson died of cancer. It felt as if the bottom of my world had fallen out.

At first I was angry – angry at God for allowing this and angry at my son and the medical profession. Slowly but surely I came to realise that bad things happen to good people and that God has never promised us a life without pain and hardship. What God did promise, though, was love enough to wipe away our tears and to hold on to us when we do not have the courage to go on.

It has taken a lot of time, and I am still recovering. But one thing I have learned is that in spite of all the bad circumstances, in spite of the pain, God is a good God who understands our pain and will never leave us or forsake us – even when it feels otherwise. All we need to do is to trust God's promises, cry out to our loving Father and persevere. When we do, we can rest in the assurance that we will one day be reunited with our loved ones. God will do the rest.

Prayer: *Father of light, we pray for all who have lost loved ones. Bring them peace and comfort. Amen*

Thought for the day: Through good and bad, God holds on to me.

Amanda Thompson (Gauteng, South Africa)

PRAYER FOCUS: PARENTS GRIEVING A CHILD

God's wings

Read Psalm 119:103–105

He will cover you with his feathers, and under his wings you will find refuge.

Psalm 91:4 (NIV)

In August 1999, while working at my job as a kindergarten teacher, I received a life-changing phone call. The doctor's receptionist said, 'Jan, the doctor needs to talk with you today, and you should bring your husband with you.' Later that day the doctor explained that I had a walnut-sized tumour growing on the lining of my brain, and it would need to be surgically removed. I was in shock and disbelief, and I was scared. But we received tremendous support as well as prayers from all around the world.

All my adult life I have read *The Upper Room* every morning. One day during the weeks before my surgery, I read a devotion based on Psalm 91:4. The image of God's wings spreading over me like a mother eagle was powerful. I carried this image with me as I prepared for surgery. As we left our home at 4.30 am to head to the hospital, I pictured God's wings over me. My surgery was successful, and the tumour was benign. Six weeks later I gratefully returned to my kindergarten students.

I learned from this experience that the Bible is not just a book filled with stories and sayings. It is God's word of compassion, love and grace to guide us to abundant life.

Prayer: *Heavenly Father, thank you for your word, which speaks to each of us. Help us as we study it to find a message of love from you. Amen*

Thought for the day: What image of God brings me comfort?

Jan Leighton (Maine, USA)

Mercy

Read Obadiah vv. 10–15

You should not gloat over your brother in the day of his misfortune, nor rejoice over the people of Judah in the day of their destruction, nor boast so much in the day of their trouble.
Obadiah v. 12 (NIV)

Have you ever disliked someone so much that you delighted in their troubles? I have. I am ashamed to admit that my 'enemy' and I are both missionaries. She runs a school through which I had hoped to obtain a visa. Her school hired me, but she and I did not get along; she fired me after six weeks. My hopes for a visa were dashed. My disappointment led to anger. Others tried to console me, but I wanted vindication, not peace.

Later, I heard that her school was having difficulties. And while I found satisfaction in her struggles, I had no peace.

Finally I remembered Obadiah's message, and I knew I needed to change. I began praying for her and her school. Slowly, as I prayed, my anger turned to mercy, and my disappointment turned to peace. As I prayed for God to bless her, God changed me so that I could genuinely rejoice in her success when her school began to prosper.

We experience God's love most fully when we pray for others to be blessed. True joy is found in God's mercy.

Prayer: *Dear God, enable us by your love to bless those who have disappointed us and to pray sincerely for our enemies. Amen*

Thought for the day: When I pray sincerely for an enemy, God can change my heart.

Andrew Michael Ardoin (Louisiana, USA)

Time is precious

Read Psalm 18:1–19

He brought me out into a spacious place; he rescued me because he delighted in me.
Psalm 18:19 (NIV)

As my grandchildren grow up, I see less and less of them. They are busy with school, friends, work and social obligations. Several weeks ago, we visited our daughter on a Sunday afternoon. Usually we catch a peek of the grandchildren as they hustle about, caught up in their activities. We always get a smile and a warm hug as they race out the door to the next thing. But this Sunday was different. They stayed home and turned off their electronic devices for the afternoon. What a blessing to spend uninterrupted time with them!

On my way home, I reflected on how I spend time with God. Sometimes I am so busy with my own life that I rush through my prayers, anxious to get on with my next activity. Sometimes I get caught up in the latest book or TV show, which cuts into the time I could spend being with God. My busyness gets in the way of experiencing God's abiding love.

I decided then to spend time with God as my grandchildren spent time with me that Sunday afternoon, just enjoying God's presence with no interruptions and no expectations. These precious visits have become the highlight of my day.

Prayer: *Dear God, thank you for always being present, even when we are too busy to notice. Help us to realise the joy of spending time in your presence. Amen*

Thought for the day: Today I will set aside distractions to spend time with God.

Jane Rager (Virginia, USA)

Faithful witness

Read Isaiah 46:3–9

'Even to your old age and grey hairs… I will sustain you.'
Isaiah 46:4 (NIV)

Even though Dad had retired, he still received frequent invitations from local churches to preach on Sundays. But when he was 89 years old, he told me that he would be preaching for the last time the following Sunday. I began making plans for the seven-hour journey to hear his final sermon.

It was an emotional service for both of us. He knew his career as a minister was ending; I knew the torch was being passed. After the call to worship and opening hymn, Dad opened his well-worn Bible. And as he did, a remarkable change took place: his voice became stronger and the words came easier. Sixty-five years of sharing God's word gave him confidence to deliver that final message; he didn't need to read the scriptures he quoted because they were written on his heart. And while his words came a bit slower and he peered at his notes a bit longer to bring them into focus, the Holy Spirit still shone through his words.

As the service ended, I knew that Dad had preached two sermons that morning: one with words and a second with his long years of faithful witness.

Prayer: *Dear God, thank you for people whose faithful lives show us how to share your good news. Amen*

Thought for the day: No matter my age, I can serve God.

JudyAnn Krell Morse (Iowa, USA)

Ravens and angels

Read Matthew 25:31–40

The ravens brought him bread and meat in the morning and bread and meat in the evening, and he drank from the brook.
1 Kings 17:6 (NIV)

I find Elijah to be one of the most interesting figures in the Bible. He suffered loneliness, persecution, humiliation and hunger in grim desert places. But God never abandoned him. God heard Elijah's pleas, saw his tears and sent ravens and angels to provide for his needs.

I can relate to Elijah's story. Recently, I was accepted into the doctoral programme at a school of theology in Colombia. The school provided a scholarship for half of my tuition. The challenge for me was to pay the remaining half as well as housing and food costs.

God, with unfailing grace, sent 'ravens and angels' – warm and gentle people – to provide meals for me. Just as people provide such care for us, we are called to be 'ravens' for others. Without a doubt, wherever we are, God counts on us to live out an authentic expression of our faith to help supply the needs of God's people.

Prayer: *Merciful God, raise our awareness of those who do not have daily bread. Multiply our efforts to help as much as we can, wherever we can, whenever we can, as we pray, 'Our Father in heaven, hallowed be your name, your kingdom come, your will be done, on earth as it is in heaven. Give us today our daily bread. And forgive us our debts, as we also have forgiven our debtors. And lead us not into temptation, but deliver us from the evil one'* Amen.*

Thought for the day: I will help another person today as God has helped me.

J. Joel Sobalvarro Nieto (Francisco Morazan, Honduras)

The light

Read John 8:12–19

The Lord is my light and salvation
Psalm 27:1 (NIV)

When the hurricane slammed into our coastal town, our family was prepared. We had stockpiled water, food, flashlights and batteries. Our children gathered in a large downstairs closet with their blankets and pillows, munching on snacks. We monitored the television coverage of the storm, hoping for the best. Although our backyard fence fell over and the wind tore at our windows, we were calm because we knew the storm would eventually pass.

Then the lights went out. The children started to cry, the television went off and the roaring of the wind seemed louder than before. In total darkness, we turned on flashlights and lit some candles. Instantly everything seemed better, our fears subsided, and we were soon talking and laughing together.

That night as I looked at my family's faces in the candlelight, I remembered how often the Bible speaks of light. The book of Genesis tells us that God created light (see Genesis 1:3). The Psalms describe the Lord as 'my light and my salvation' (Psalm 27:1). In the gospels we hear Jesus proclaim, 'I am the light of the world' (John 8:12). The lights went out in our house during the storm, but God's light will never go out in our lives. If we follow Christ, we will never walk in darkness.

Prayer: *Dear God, thank you for filling our lives with your light. Amen*

Thought for the day: God is my light.

Kathleen Harder (Texas, USA)

PRAYER FOCUS: DISASTER-RELIEF WORKERS

Poor reception

Read Luke 11:5–13

*Where can I go from your Spirit? Where can I flee from your presence?
If I go up to the heavens, you are there; if I make my bed in the depths,
you are there.*

Psalm 139:7–8 (NIV)

Being unfamiliar with modern phones, I asked my son to get for me one that he thought would best suit me. When I visited him to pick it up, I decided to try it out while I was sat with him, to get used to how it worked. I called his phone, but it didn't connect. I tried sending a text message, but that did not go through either.

I told my son the phone would have to go back, as it didn't work. He laughed and said that the phone was fine. The problem was he lived in an area with poor mobile reception – some days it was good; other days they could not get any signal. Sure enough, when I got home and tried again, I was able to reach him, though the line was not very clear.

I reflected on this. Here I had a brand new, up-to-date phone. Yes, with this phone I could ring home from anywhere in the world, but only if I had a good signal, kept it charged up and didn't lose it or have it stolen. What a relief, I thought, that we do not have this trouble when contacting God. No matter where I go, from the deepest of caves to the highest of mountains, his signal is always clear.

It's awesome to think that all of us, at any time and anywhere, can call upon our Father in heaven, the creator of the universe. Indeed, as Jesus taught us, we can ask, seek and knock, knowing that we will receive, find and that the door will be opened.

Prayer: *Loving Father, let us know that we are never on our own when we know you.*

Thought for the day: God is only a thought away, day or night.

Brian Gaunt (England, United Kingdom)

A broken world

Read Psalm 119:1–16

I have hidden your word in my heart that I might not sin against you.
Psalm 119:11 (NIV)

'It's broken!' Tears streamed down my child's face as water poured out of his snow globe, and the world inside was destroyed. This small toy, which had brought him so much joy, could not be fixed and now was a source of sorrow. I think that this is probably a bit of how God feels seeing the brokenness of our world. But unlike my son's snow globe, our world isn't being thrown away. God has a plan to redeem it, one that's already been put in motion through the birth, death and resurrection of Jesus Christ.

My son's broken snow globe was edged with glass and too dangerous to be kept. Likewise, our world is filled with sin, which brings danger with it. But God does not abandon us. Today's verse makes it sound simple: learn God's word and avoid sin. But while it may be simple, it's not easy. Although it's not always easy to get up early each morning to spend time with God, every time I do my day is better for it. God's word helps us grow in faith and reassures us that God is redeeming the brokenness of the world.

Prayer: *Dear God, thank you for the gift of your word. Help us to grow in our relationship with you. Amen*

Thought for the day: Reading God's word reminds me that God loves the world.

T. L. Valluy (Île-de-France, France)

Compassionate listening

Read Hebrews 13:1–6

Continue to remember those in prison as if you were together with them in prison, and those who are ill-treated as if you yourselves were suffering.

Hebrews 13:3 (NIV)

Less than one month into my first job as a prison chaplain, a man caught my attention as I was walking by. He looked young, and his smile seemed forced. As we sat at cold metal tables, this young man told me of the devastating life circumstances that had led him to addiction and criminal behavior. As I told him of God's extravagant forgiveness, I watched his tired smile turn to tears of joyful repentance. He received Christ into his heart that day.

God calls us to give ear to the plight of those in prison. Separated from loved ones and removed from home and community, those in prison can feel isolated and forgotten. Rather than ignore or condemn those who are incarcerated, we are called to have compassion and offer a listening ear. We can share with them the hope we find through our faith through prison pen pal programmes or by volunteering in local prison ministries.

There are countless people behind bars, both literal and figurative, who need our listening ears and tender hearts. As we remember to love those in prison, God will set their souls free.

Prayer: *Dear Lord, help us to have compassion for those who are incarcerated and to share with them the hope of the gospel. In Jesus' name. Amen*

Thought for the day: How can I share God's love with someone in prison?

Pierce VanDunk (Massachusetts, USA)

Beyond all understanding

Read Philippians 4:4–7

The peace of God, which surpasses all understanding, will guard your hearts and your minds in Christ Jesus.
Philippians 4:7 (NRSV)

As a recent university graduate, I was anxious about my future. I was uncertain about how best to teach my dance students, worried about family members' health issues and overwhelmed by chores. I was in a bad mood.

On the drive to a nice lunch with my mum and brother, with hope that some nourishment might put me in a better frame of mind, I prayed repeatedly for God's peace. But I got frustrated when I couldn't seem to gain a feeling of inner tranquillity.

Our definition of peace generally means complete contentedness along with the absence of troubles. It is how I feel at the beach, lying on the soft sand without a care in the world while the sun warms my body and a breeze gently cools it.

But then I remembered that God's peace is more than a feeling. As today's verse reminds us, God's peace goes beyond all human understanding. Even amid restlessness and anxiety about our lives and responsibilities, our faith promises God's presence, help and grace. God's peace is not confined to feelings. God extends peace to us even when – and especially when – we can't seem to find tranquillity.

Prayer: *Dear Lord, help us to remember that your peace is present amid our anxieties and uncertainties, waiting for us to take hold of it. Amen*

Thought for the day: When I am anxious, God offers me peace.

Mikaela Horvath (California, USA)

PRAYER FOCUS: RECENT UNIVERSITY GRADUATES

Reminders of God

Read Psalm 19:1–9

Give thanks to the God of heaven – God's faithful love lasts forever!
Psalm 136:26 (CEB)

Like many families, we have photos scattered throughout our home. Most of the time they become an unnoticed part of the background, but every now and then I stop to appreciate them. They remind me of happy times and of the life stages that our children and grandchildren have passed through. Some of the photos are of special occasions like weddings or a first day of school; some were posed and others were taken on the go. Each one is special.

Photos can stir memories and be appreciated again and again, and they can even be shared with friends who visit. Our photos remind me of the smiles, mannerisms, special qualities and kindness of family members who no longer live nearby or who have died. It is a joy to remember those loved ones when I see my photos.

Like the photos around my house, reminders of God are scattered around me too, though I often fail to notice. I can see God's beauty and bounty when I wander around my garden. I can catch glimpses of God's love when I am with friends. And the Bible tells me how much God loves me and wants me to love God in return. May we always appreciate the nearness and love of God and share that love with others.

Prayer: *Loving Father, thank you for the many glimpses of you that we can find every day. Help us to share your love with others. Amen*

Thought for the day: Where have I seen reminders of God today?

Meg Mangan (New South Wales, Australia)

Nurturing love

Read 1 Corinthians 2:9–13

'What no eye has seen, what no ear has heard, and what no human mind has conceived' – the things God has prepared for those who love him.
1 Corinthians 2:9 (NIV)

Six months after I lost my wife of 43 years to cancer, I was still grieving. Heartbreak and depression lingered with me daily. My church family was supportive, and my pastor had counselled and consoled me. Then Pastor Tom asked if I would talk about my experience of loss in the church during a Sunday service.

When I saw Pastor Tom a few days later, I told him I didn't feel worthy to share my story with the congregation. Without hesitation, he offered a warm, knowing smile and said, 'Mike, you may not be worthy, but God is and Jesus Christ is!' That moment was an awakening. I had been looking for relief and healing in myself, my job and other worldly distractions. In just one simple sentence, Pastor Tom reminded me that I could let God's love and healing power lead me.

God sent Jesus Christ to give me a new life, so I can be assured, be confident and let others know the good news. This simple truth has helped me transition from the grief and sadness of my loss to positive spiritual growth. I participate in activities with my church family, I pray daily, I study my faith in Bible classes and I acknowledge the blessings of the Lord at work in my life every day. My strength grows and life has become more meaningful. I am a testament to God's nurturing love.

Prayer: *Father God, show us the way. Teach us to set aside our self-centred ways and to focus on you. Amen*

Thought for the day: In our grief we can find healing by sharing God's love.

Mike Starry (Virginia, USA)

PRAYER FOCUS: SOMEONE WHO IS NEWLY WIDOWED

The landscape of life

Read Deuteronomy 11:8–15

Beloved, let us love one another, because love is from God; everyone who loves is born of God and knows God.
1 John 4:7 (NRSV)

Walking through the pasture on an early spring day, I noticed all the tender new sprouts pushing their way through the rich soil. At my feet were hundreds of tiny flowers in shades of yellow, white and lavender. Some could have been considered weeds, while others held the promise of lush green grass. Across the expanse, a blanket of colour spread out before me. All the rainbow colours of the field fit together to paint a beautiful landscape.

God is the painter of the landscape around me – flowers, trees, hills. God has also placed before me a landscape of people of many colours and backgrounds, each as tender as the sprouts of spring. But how easily we fail to delight in this landscape as much as we do in the rich array of colours in the pastures or on the hillsides! If, however, we recognise each person as a child of God and show each one God's grace, we can be in awe of the variety of God's creation visible in humankind.

Jesus taught us to love one another, including those who annoy, aggravate and disagree with us. Many problems of our world can be solved if we find ways to love our neighbours as ourselves.

Prayer: *God of creation, thank you for the beauty of the earth and of your people. Help us love one another as you have loved us. In Jesus' name. Amen*

Thought for the day: Each person I encounter is a precious child of God.

Kim Sisk (Oklahoma, USA)

A green ribbon

Read Psalm 133

Glorify the Lord with me: let us exalt his name together.
Psalm 34:3 (NIV)

After one of my meditations appeared in *Csendes Percek*, the Hungarian edition of *The Upper Room*, I received a letter. It was from an 86-year-old woman who had read my meditation, noticed that we lived nearby and wanted to connect. Since then, we've met in person and have kept in contact over the phone and through letters.

One day, another of my meditations appeared in the magazine. It was about a Bible camp where campers donned different coloured ribbons – children wore orange ribbons, adults wore green. I wrote about how we are always growing spiritually, and I wondered what colour ribbon would represent my level of spiritual maturity. Would it be green to indicate a mature faith that is still growing?

That day I got a call from my letter-writing friend. With enthusiasm, she said, 'I understood the message about the ribbon, and I wanted to let you know that I'm doing my chores with a green ribbon on my wrist.' What a wonderful affirmation! I put on my green ribbon as encouragement for my spiritual journey. I believe God rejoices when we share our testimonies. Witnessing for God strengthens our faith and encourages others in theirs.

Prayer: *Heavenly Father, thank you for our spiritual brothers and sisters. Help us not to miss opportunities to share your love with others. Amen*

Thought for the day: Who needs to hear my testimony today?

Pál Tünde (Pest, Hungary)

PRAYER FOCUS: CHRISTIAN WRITERS

The woodpecker

Read Romans 15:1–13

*Whatever was written in the past was written for our instruction
so that we could have hope through endurance and through the
encouragement of the scriptures.*
Romans 15:4 (CEB)

I heard it again. I woke up to the same sound that I had heard every
morning for the previous three weeks: *da, da, da, da, da* in rapid suc-
cession. When I first heard it, I had a suspicion that I knew the source
of the noise. When I ventured outside to confirm my suspicion, I found
that a woodpecker, with its characteristic red stripe, had discovered a
power pole that must have been full of insects. The woodpecker would
stay there the entire day, driving its beak into the wood again and again
feeding on the bugs.

Reflecting on the woodpecker's behaviour, I had to ask myself a question: 'Do I linger in God's word with the same kind of dedication and
focus as the woodpecker does on this power pole?' The wooden pole
houses rich nutrients for this bird, and I know that the Bible grants me
wisdom for my life. Perhaps I need to be as consistent in pursuing its
offerings.

A centuries-old practice called *lectio divina* helps me explore God's
word more deeply. Reading each Bible verse or story four times, inter-
spersed with pausing and reflecting, prompts me to discern and savour
God's message in truly profound ways. And whenever I hear the woodpecker, I thank him for this reminder.

Prayer: *Dear Lord, we need you. Help us to discern the wisdom of your
word by reading it daily and savouring it. In Jesus' name. Amen*

Thought for the day: I can go deeper into God's word by pondering
each verse.

Mark de Roo (Michigan, USA)

Now and always

Read Matthew 4:1–11

He answered, 'It is written, "One does not live by bread alone, but by every word that comes from the mouth of God."'
Matthew 4:4 (NRSV)

The Covid-19 pandemic filled me with anxiety. The waiting and disruption of normal life made me think of the time when my friend Jane, a hair stylist, injured both hands and became unable to work. In addition to not earning money, Jane couldn't cook or clean or do much of anything else. Her sons helped around the house, but Jane's doctors told her she would have to wait and see if her hands would heal. Jane didn't know what to do, so she started spending hours each day praying and reading scripture. After about two years, her hands did heal and she was able to return to work.

Jane didn't know how long she would have to wait for healing, just as we don't know how long it will be before our lives can return to 'normal'. And as we ponder Jesus' wilderness experience, it occurs to me that the Bible doesn't say whether Jesus knew how long he would have to endure his time of temptation. Did he also experience the anxiety of the unknown?

The one thing we do know is that God is with us – now and always. And like Jane, we can pray and read scripture. My prayers may be as much complaint and lament as gratitude and joy, but communicating with God and meditating on God's word always make me feel better.

Prayer: *Dear God, thank you for being with us in the wilderness. Help us to keep in touch with you and to share your love with others. In Jesus' name we pray. Amen*

Thought for the day: Talking with God and reading the Bible helps me get through the day.

Marilyn Dorn (Virginia, USA)

PRAYER FOCUS: SOMEONE WHO CANNOT WORK DUE TO INJURY

Unique

Read 1 Samuel 16:1–13

I praise you, for I am fearfully and wonderfully made. Wonderful are your works; that I know very well.
Psalm 139:14 (NRSV)

As a five-foot-tall teenager with a poor complexion, I was always on the receiving end of jokes. My so-called friends called me by nicknames that referenced my height, and my well-meaning relatives recommended creams for my skin and exercises to help me grow taller. All this depressed me to no end. Then I went to a new city for school, and people started recognising me for my academic abilities. It was a turning point for me.

Because I was focused on my strengths and abilities, I was no longer bothered by what I did not have. I was able to laugh along with people who made fun of my height. Ever since, I have made it a point to counsel people, especially kids who are bullied for their appearance. God has used me and blessed me wonderfully.

As we read in 1 Samuel 16, while we see outward appearances, the Lord looks at the heart. There are many instances in the Bible where God used a variety of different people for God's glory – Moses, Samson, Mary, Zacchaeus. It's easy to concentrate on what we do not have, but let us praise God for the wonderful life we have been given and use it to God's glory.

Prayer: *Dear God, thank you for the unique talents that you have given each of us. Use us to bring you glory. In Jesus' name we pray. Amen*

Thought for the day: I am special because God made me.

Sahana Mathias (Karnataka, India)

Always with us

Read Psalm 62:1–8

The Lord your God is in your midst… He will create calm with his love;
he will rejoice over you with singing.
Zephaniah 3:17 (CEB)

When my wife and I babysit our granddaughter, she doesn't always cooperate when it is time for her to go to bed. She cries as we put her in her cot in unfamiliar surroundings. I sit next to her cot in the dark, patting her back and soothing her until she settles and her cries diminish. From time to time, not fully asleep, she'll glance up to see if I'm still there, watching her, protecting her, ready to soothe and comfort her. Eventually she goes to sleep, content and relaxed.

The way she peeks to see if I am still there reminds me of God's constant presence in our lives. Sometimes we are uncertain of God's presence and try to get a glimpse of God. When we're in the dark and desperate for soothing and support, God is there. In whatever circumstances we find ourselves – no matter how dark – we can trust in God's promise to be with us.

Prayer: *Dear Father, thank you for your presence with us, even in the toughest times. Amen*

Thought for the day: Even in my darkest moments, I can find rest in God's presence.

Kevin McPoyle (Pennsylvania, USA)

Beyond words

Read Romans 8:26–28

The Spirit helps us in our weakness; for we do not know how to pray as we ought, but that very Spirit intercedes with sighs too deep for words.

Romans 8:26 (NRSV)

One morning during the winter of 2011, I woke unable to speak. I panicked because I worked as a professional singer and voice-over artist. Little did I know it would be four months before I would be able to speak again, let alone sing. What was eventually diagnosed as a perfect storm of viral laryngitis, acid reflux and muscle tension ended my singing career and threatened my very sense of self. Who was I and what was my purpose if God could no longer use me to sing and speak to others?

One afternoon I came across Paul's words to the Romans describing how the Holy Spirit helps us when we feel weak. I was overcome by the realisation that God is able to work in and through us all, regardless of our human limitations.

My voice eventually returned, but I no longer feel dependent upon it to do God's work. I have been inspired by the many circumstances in which people serve God. As Paul writes, 'All things work together for good for those who love God, who are called according to his purpose.' Perhaps we can all learn that God can use all things in our lives for good and that we will always have purpose.

Prayer: *Dear God, thank you for being able to use everything for good – even our weaknesses and trials. May we allow the Holy Spirit to work through us to do your work. Amen*

Thought for the day: There are many ways for me to serve God.

Jennifer McCluskey (Virginia, USA)

Called to serve

Read Matthew 9:37–38

Let us not become weary in doing good, for at the proper time we will reap a harvest if we do not give up. Therefore, as we have opportunity, let us do good to all people, especially to those who belong to the family of believers.

Galatians 6:9–10 (NIV)

After attending a meeting that included a presentation on mission work in the Dominican Republic, I began to pray for those involved. A few years later, I vacationed in the Dominican Republic. A pastor friend of mine travelled four hours to my hotel to take me to his local church to preach. As we walked through the community, I was shocked to see the material and spiritual poverty. My spirit was troubled. I could sense the Holy Spirit admonishing me for staying in a luxury hotel, wasting money while people nearby lived lives of poverty and hopelessness.

After that day I became actively involved in mission work. With God's help, our teams have shared the love and hope of Jesus Christ with hundreds of people in the Dominican Republic, Haiti and Guatemala. My constant prayer is to seek God's guidance and to continue to serve. As I serve the Lord, I am grateful for the blessing of God's love and forgiveness.

Prayer: *God of all, inspire us in ordinary and extraordinary ways. Help us to heed your call to live out the good news of Jesus Christ to care for and serve all those in need. Amen*

Thought for the day: The abundance God has given me is meant to be shared.

Ariel Rivera García (Puerto Rico, USA)

Not fear but love

Read 2 Timothy 1:3–7

God hath not given us the spirit of fear; but of power, and of love, and of a sound mind.
2 Timothy 1:7 (KJV)

For 45 years I have been friends with a woman from Turkey who is Muslim. Her husband came to the US for medical school, and they now live in Istanbul. My friend Berrin and I have prayed for each other and our families for many years. We have visited them in Turkey, and they have come to Nebraska to visit us several times.

Recently, Berrin was told she has cancer. I wish I could be with her to help. Because of my own health issues, I can't travel that far anymore. At times my fears for her are overwhelming.

In my prayer time, I have read and reread the words from 2 Timothy above. When I meditate on these words, I like to picture placing my prayer requests at the feet of Jesus. This practice helps me calm my fears and keep my trust in Jesus. I write several of my favourite verses on a card. Then I tuck them into my Bible so that I read them first. In so doing, I am able to begin my Bible reading and prayer in a more peaceful and trusting way.

I love my dear friend Berrin. I know God loves her too. I can rest assured that she is in God's healing arms, and so I am at peace. We can all find calm amid our fears when we put our trust in God.

Prayer: *Heavenly Father, help us to place our fears at your feet as we face illness. Help us to entrust those we love to your care. Amen*

Thought for the day: When I give my fears to God, I can find peace.

Nancy R. Meyer (Nebraska, USA)

Flourishing again

Read Psalm 63

'Be strong and courageous. Do not be afraid or terrified because of them, for the Lord your God goes with you; he will never leave you nor forsake you.'
Deuteronomy 31:6 (NIV)

Every winter, I spend four months living in Mexico City and working at two refugee centres. In May, before returning home, I spend a week on Mexico's southwest beach coast.

May is the end of a nearly six-month dry season, and almost all of the trees are stripped of their leaves. The landscape is gray, and the soil is hard and dry. If they could, the trees might ask, 'Where are you, God?' However one tree, the cuachalalate, starts producing small white flowers. In the harsh dryness that dominates the area in May, this tree begins to thrive.

Every year I marvel at this new life and am reminded that we all experience seasons of spiritual dryness. I know that shortly after I leave Mexico, the rains will begin and the parched countryside will flourish once again. I also know that if I wait patiently and listen for God's still small voice, God's love will always lead me home.

Even if it feels like we are alone, God never leaves us, just as God never leaves that arid Mexican countryside. As Deuteronomy 31:6 promises, 'The Lord… will never leave you nor forsake you.'

Prayer: *Gracious God, may we never forget that you are always present. Thank you for your love that guides us. Amen*

Thought for the day: No matter the circumstances, God's love enables me to flourish.

Daniel Ladue (New York, USA)

Loaves and fishes

Read John 6:5–13

'Here is a boy with five small barley loaves and two small fish, but how far will they go among so many?'
John 6:9 (NIV)

I noticed a need at my new church: a choir to lead congregational hymn singing. Although I've been part of church choirs since my childhood, the idea of directing an adult choir scared me. Yet when I mentioned the need to the elders, they asked me to organise and lead a choir. If I said yes, I risked failing in front of the whole church.

In today's reading, a few fish and small barley loaves, offered by a young boy, looked foolish and inadequate compared to a hungry multitude. However, in the hands of Jesus, everyone had enough to eat. When I offered my limited musical skill, God made it enough to form a choir. Our congregation that used to stumble through hymns without a choir to lead us now sings with confidence.

We encounter different needs every day. Sometimes we might think, 'Somebody should do something about that.' Maybe we are that somebody. Are we willing to risk failure by stepping into a task that seems impossible? The Bible is full of people who risked looking foolish and failing. Noah, Gideon, Esther and David all did impossible things with God's help. And we can too.

Prayer: *Heavenly Father, the need is great, and we are small. With your help, all things are possible. In Jesus' name, we pray. Amen*

Thought for the day: God can multiply my small offering to meet the needs of many.

Jane Reid (Oregon, USA)

Sleeping soundly

Read Psalm 3

I lie down and sleep; I wake again, because the Lord sustains me. I will not fear though tens of thousands assail me on every side.
Psalm 3:5–6 (NIV)

Some time ago, I had trouble sleeping for several nights. After sleeping only one or two hours, I kept waking up. I remembered a friend once said, 'If someone wakes up several times in the night, maybe they are stressed.' It was true that during that time I had many problems, but I didn't think too much of them. One afternoon when I was alone in the upper room of my house, I felt a longing in my heart to worship God. Immediately I raised my voice in praise. That night, I slept soundly.

I might have felt like I was not thinking about my problems, but actually my soul was miserable. By praising and worshipping God, my soul was strengthened. It was as if my dry soul had been watered, and like David I could say, 'I lie down and sleep… because the Lord sustains me.' Our worries may not disappear when we worship God, but they lose their power when we arrive in God's presence.

Prayer: *Loving God, even in the midst of our problems, help us to sing songs of praise to you. We pray as Jesus taught us, 'Father, hallowed be your name, your kingdom come. Give us each day our daily bread. Forgive us our sins, for we also forgive everyone who sins against us. And lead us not into temptation.'**

Thought for the day: When I praise and worship God, I can find strength to face any problem.

Linawati Santoso (East Java, Indonesia)

PRAYER FOCUS: THOSE WHO HAVE INSOMNIA

*Luke 11:2–4

Finding our way home

Read Matthew 11:25–30

'Take my yoke upon you and learn from me, for I am gentle and humble in heart, and you will find rest for your souls. For my yoke is easy and my burden is light.'
Matthew 11:29–30 (NIV)

Living in southern Arizona gives me the opportunity to enjoy summer hiking on cool mountain trails and winter hiking on warm desert paths. One autumn day I was hiking alone on a trail, following a mountain stream. Even though I was carrying a heavy backpack, I was caught up in the beauty of the colourful autumn leaves of the oak, ash and cottonwood trees.

While exploring this beauty, I left the path and became disoriented. I began to feel a sense of panic, and my pack now seemed much heavier. How quickly I had gone from the euphoria of a beautiful day to the shock and exhaustion of being lost. Because of my outdoor training I calmed myself, pulled out my compass, reoriented myself and got back on the right path. Somehow my heavy backpack seemed lighter again, and I felt refreshed as I safely returned home.

The correct path was safe and beautiful, but I ran into trouble as soon as I decided to find my own way. My experience reminded me that when I spend time daily, reading scripture and building my relationship with the living Lord, I am refreshed and always able to find my way home.

Prayer: *Gracious God, thank you for your beautiful creation and for the divine guidance you have shared with us through the Bible. Thank you for showing us the way home through your risen son, Jesus Christ. Amen*

Thought for the day: Reading the Bible daily guides me on life's path.

Doug Wingert (Arizona, USA)

Finishing well

Read Romans 5:1–8

I have fought the good fight, I have finished the race, I have kept the faith.
2 Timothy 4:7 (NIV)

At the 1968 Olympic Games in Mexico City, John Stephen Akhwari was a marathon runner for Tanzania. During the race he fell, dislocating his knee and injuring his shoulder. In spite of his injuries he finished the race, although he was an hour behind the winner. When later he was asked by the press why he didn't give up, he replied, 'My country did not send me 5,000 miles to start the race; they sent me 5,000 miles to finish the race.'

My motto at school was a Latin phrase that means 'The end crowns the work.' I understood it this way: 'If you work to the end, you will win the crown.' Those words have encouraged me all my life.

Finishing well with perseverance was one of the themes of the apostle Paul, who wrote, 'We know that suffering produces perseverance; perseverance, character; and character, hope.' Then at the end of his life, Paul was able to write these words: 'I have finished the race, I have kept the faith. Now there is in store for me the crown of righteousness' (2 Timothy 4:7–8).

We don't need to be marathon runners or the apostle Paul to finish this life well. By keeping our eyes on Jesus, we can hear him say, 'Well done, good and faithful servant!' (Matthew 25:21).

Prayer: *O Lord, we pray that we may finish well and win the crown of life with you. Amen*

Thought for the day: Faithful living allows me to finish life's race well.

Carol Purves (England, United Kingdom)

Waves of trouble

Read Psalm 46:1–6

God is our refuge and strength, an ever-present help in trouble.
Psalm 46:1 (NIV)

One day at the beach, not long after I placed my chair at the edge of the water, a father and his young son ventured into the ocean. The boy frolicked in the gentle lapping waves. Because the tide was coming in, the waves soon became much larger. One wave caught the young boy off guard, and he lost his balance. His dad sprang into action and helped him regain composure. As quickly as the wave had appeared, it diminished into the shoreline and the boy ran from his dad's protection with newfound confidence. It was not long until a similarly threatening wave appeared; however, the boy had learned from his experience. He ran to his dad, wrapped his small arms around one of his dad's legs, and rode out the crashing wave in safety. The boy knew where to turn for help.

This cycle repeated itself several times, and I realised that life has a lot of waves that come at us. Some of the waves are easy to withstand, but some of them knock us off balance. Whom do we turn to when a wave hits? Do we try to brave the rough waters alone? God is watching us and waiting to offer protection and comfort. We can hold on to God as the waves crash around us.

Prayer: *Dear God, thank you for always being here for us. Help us to turn quickly to you in times of trouble. We need not try to keep our balance on our own. Amen*

Thought for the day: In times of trouble, I will hold on to God.

Michelle T. Johnson (North Carolina, USA)

Sent to encourage

Read Luke 2:8–15

Do not neglect to show hospitality to strangers, for by doing that some have entertained angels without knowing it.
Hebrews 13:2 (NRSV)

I had just completed four hours of medication infusion to treat my lymphoma. Like every treatment, it had left me fatigued. My wife and I drove to a nearby restaurant to await the 4.00 pm opening time.

Two women were already sitting on the long bench outside and graciously welcomed us to join them. As we waited to enter the restaurant, one of the women asked, 'Are you all from this area?' With my weakened voice I replied, 'No, we come from the east coast for my cancer treatments here.' She identified herself as a Christian and said that she would like to pray for me. She took my hand, raised it up with hers and interceded fervently to God for help, hope and healing for me.

After four or five minutes of ardent praying, she concluded, 'In Jesus' great name!' Then she said, 'My name is Angel; what's yours?' I replied, 'Bill, and like you I am a Christian. I pray the Lord's special blessing on you – because this day you have met and ministered to me unexpectedly.' I never saw that woman again, but I know that God sent her to encourage me.

Prayer: *O God, help us not only to receive strangers but also to respond with humility and thanksgiving when you send them to minister to us unexpectedly. Amen*

Thought for the day: Today I will look for someone who needs my prayers.

Bill Weimer (Florida, USA)

Provided for

Read 2 Corinthians 9:6–15

Whoever is kind to the poor lends to the Lord, and will be repaid in full.
Proverbs 19:17 (NRSV)

I first met Mzee in a hotel. His eyes were sunken, his back was bent and he was walking with the support of a stick. I was moved with compassion as I watched him order a cup of tea. Later on, I inquired as to who he was and where he lived. A young man took me to Mzee's home, and I could not believe what I saw. He was sitting alone in front of his house. The roof and the walls were made of grass, and the walls had holes large enough for a person to fit through. I learned that his wife and relatives had deserted him, leaving him to struggle to provide for himself in his old age. Around his house, I could see the small gardens he cultivated. I decided to offer him food each week, even though I don't have much myself.

The seed I have been sowing may seem small, but it is helping Mzee. For this I am glad, and recently I have seen God providing for me in a similar way. When my friend came to stay for two weeks, she gave me money to buy groceries and helped me pay for other things as well. Before she left, she asked if she could continue to send me money for groceries. Just as God prompted me to help Mzee, I believe that through my friend, God is helping me.

Prayer: *Dear God, help us to be willing to share what you have given us with those who have less. In Jesus' name. Amen*

Thought for the day: I can help provide for others in the way God provides for me.

Enid Adah Nyinomujuni (Dar es Salaam, Tanzania)

Faith like a child

Read Matthew 18.1–5

'Truly I tell you, unless you change and become like little children, you will never enter the kingdom of heaven.'
Matthew 18:3 (NIV)

It is easy to forget what it was like to have the faith of a child. When I look back at my life, I tend to remember what my life was like after I decided to follow Jesus when I was 17 – no longer a child.

It was not until I began working in a Christian school that I began to understand what it means to have faith like a child. Being around children aged three to 14 has opened my eyes to Jesus' teaching in Matthew. Whenever I pray with my students, they always pray for other people and their needs. On one of my first days at the school, a seven-year old prayed for his pet that had fleas. These kids trust that God is close and listening. They don't get caught up in picking the right or best words, sounding eloquent or what others think of their prayer. Instead they are sincere and present in the moment in a way that I envy.

It is easy for me to get lost in worry about the future, to pray only for my needs without seeking a real encounter with God. When we think back on what it was like to be a child and look at the children around us, we can learn much from those expressions of faith.

Prayer: *Heavenly Father, help us to be truly your children, trusting in you and your care for us today and always. Amen*

Thought for the day: I can learn much from the faith of children around me.

Paul Cillo (Pennsylvania, USA)

PRAYER FOCUS: SCHOOL CHILDREN

Purpose

Read Psalm 57:1–5

I cry to God Most High, to God who fulfills his purpose for me.
Psalm 57:2 (NRSV)

When I was diagnosed with cancer at age 17, it came as a total shock. My friends were taking placement tests and applying for college scholarships while I was fighting for my life. Although cancer was scary, I felt a quiet confidence that I would survive. As I counted down the days until my final treatment, I began to dream about my future and wonder how God would use my sickness for good.

Several years later, a national cancer charity offered me a job connecting and supporting other cancer survivors across the country. When I shared my personal story, it gave other survivors hope. I'd often reflect on how God steered me in a direction where I could use my experience fighting cancer to encourage others. I found purpose despite all of the pain.

In today's reading, King David has experienced a disaster – his life was also at stake. Yet as he struggled, he took refuge in God, and by doing so he remembered that God had a purpose for his life.

When we find ourselves facing disaster, we may be tempted to lose trust in the promise that God has good plans for us. But scripture reminds us that God can work through our struggles to bring our purpose to light.

Prayer: *Father God, help us to take refuge in you and remember that our lives have purpose when we live them following you. Amen*

Thought for the day: God has a purpose for my life.

Danielle Ripley-Burgess (Missouri, USA)

Never alone

Read Joshua 1:1–9

'Have I not commanded you? Be strong and courageous. Do not be afraid; do not be discouraged, for the Lord your God will be with you wherever you go.'
Joshua 1:9 (NIV)

My daily commute to work consists of a 25-minute drive, one way, on a rural two-lane road. Even though most days are trouble-free, problems such as wildlife crossing the road, downed trees and flooded roadways are always possible. The biggest challenge is when winter brings a mess of snow, ice and wind. On those days I drive well under the speed limit as I carefully make my way up and down the snow-covered hills.

One day it occurred to me that my winter drive is similar to life. The icy roads and snowy hills are comparable to life's troubles – the death of a family member, the loss of a job, a devastating health diagnosis. Just as I don't know what lies ahead on my journey, as we travel through life we don't know what awaits us either.

One thing we know for sure is this promise from Jesus: 'In this world you will have trouble. But take heart! I have overcome the world' (John 16:33). Jesus didn't promise us an easy life, but he told us not to worry because no matter how hard our journey is, he has already won the fight. So when we find ourselves sliding along life's roadway, worrying about the future, we can find comfort and peace in knowing that Jesus is with us on the journey.

Prayer: *Heavenly Father, help us to remember that no matter how troubling life gets, you are always with us. In Jesus' name. Amen*

Thought for the day: I can take heart because Jesus is with me on the journey.

Jordan S. Hiquet (Pennsylvania, USA)

PRAYER FOCUS: THOSE WHO TRAVEL DANGEROUS ROADS TO WORK

Our shepherd

Read Psalm 23
The Lord is my shepherd, I shall not want.
Psalm 23:1 (NRSV)

On a recent bicycle ride I spotted a flock of sheep. They were quite calm and appeared to be resting. None seemed nervous. 'This image,' I thought, 'can be an example for us as children of God.'

In reality, sometimes our circumstances infringe upon our peace and rob us of tranquillity. For many reasons, worries and fears may overwhelm us in different situations. Uncertainty can weigh heavily on us and keep us from enjoying the calm and peace that I saw in that flock of sheep.

But the picture of God described by the psalmist in Psalm 23 remains true for us today: God will care for us, offer us rest, protect us from harm and supply our needs. We can be sure that when we place our trust in the Lord as our shepherd, we will lack nothing.

Prayer: *Dear Lord, help us to place our complete trust in you and find rest in your promises. In the name of Jesus, we pray. Amen*

Thought for the day: Today I will place my trust in God, our shepherd.

Lilia Roberts (Chubut, Argentina)

Oneness in Christ

Read Romans 12:1–8

In Christ we, though many, form one body, and each member belongs to all the others.
Romans 12:5 (NIV)

I am from a culture in which people do not readily share their deeper concerns or joys. Out of fear of having their 'business on the streets', people endure silently. And out of fear of not respecting another's difficulties, they hesitate to celebrate their joys. This situation deprives the community of the most joyful and saddest life-changing events.

Some months ago, when our daughter was diagnosed with a heart condition, we shared with and invited prayers from members of our ministry community around the world. On the day of the surgery, phone calls and text messages brought us words of assurance and reminders of prayerful support from friends everywhere. We knew that a community of believers surrounded us and that they were channelling God's grace to our family and to the medical team. It made a huge difference, and we were at peace.

Today's reading from Romans 12 reminds me of the wholeness we find in community. With all our imperfections, we are each a special gift to one another. Offering our deepest concerns and joys to our community can be challenging, but it is part of God's call on our life. We draw closer to God as we develop and work through our relationships with others.

Prayer: *Liberating God, set us free to trust that as we share our joys and sorrows with others, we will all be brought closer to you in community. Amen*

Thought for the day: My community is a gift from God.

Stephane Brooks (Tennessee, USA)

With us always

Read Matthew 28:16–20

'Remember, I am with you always, to the end of the age.'
Matthew 28:20 (NRSV)

When I took my two-year-old grandson Samuel to a preschool playgroup for the first time, he loved it! Samuel was enjoying himself until he suddenly realised he could not see me. He ran to the centre of the room with a look of panic on his face as he scanned around, searching. I called to him, but in the busyness of the room, he couldn't find me. Anxiously, Samuel called out, 'Grandma!' Immediately I went up and hugged him, reassuring him that I hadn't left him. Comforted, Samuel was soon off playing happily again.

Later as I reflected on Samuel's moment of panic, I realised that I also get overwhelmed at times. I can be too distracted by circumstances to recognise God's presence. In those moments I look around wondering where God is, when in reality God is right there with me. When Jesus gave the disciples the great commission, he also reassured them saying, 'Remember, I am with you always, to the end of the age.' That promise holds true for us today. What a comfort it is to know that no matter what happens or how bleak life may seem, we are safe under the Lord's care.

Prayer: *Thank you, Lord, for never leaving us alone. Help us to remember that you are always with us, especially when life feels scary. Amen*

Thought for the day: The Lord is with me, today and every day.

Devona R. Allison (Florida, USA)

In God's presence

Read 1 Kings 19:6–18

After the wind there was an earthquake, but the Lord was not in the earthquake. After the earthquake came a fire, but the Lord was not in the fire. And after the fire came a gentle whisper.

1 Kings 19:11–12 (NIV)

Tonight, I watched the sunset from the middle of the lake in a red canoe. Behind me the sky was a hazy purple; in front of me, bright orange and peach. Stillness enveloped me, with only the sounds of the wild echoing around me. It was as if the Lord were inviting me to be still. In the silence I felt God speak to my heart, saying, 'Trust me. Surrender to me.' The weight of all my burdens lifted as I sat with God.

I was reminded of Elijah's encounter with God in 1 Kings 19. Elijah did not find the Lord in the mighty wind, in the earthquake or in the fire. Elijah's encounter with God came in the gentle whisper, in the stillness. Often, I look for God in the big things, but perhaps God is best found when I quiet my thoughts and humble my heart before God. I think being in the Lord's presence is one of the greatest treasures we will ever know.

Prayer: *Dear Lord, teach us to be still before you and to humble our hearts so that we may rest in your presence. Amen*

Thought for the day: How often do I accept God's invitation to sit and to be still?

Tina Claxton (Ontario, Canada)

I am. I will.

Read Isaiah 41:1–14

Do not fear, for I am with you; do not be dismayed, for I am your God. I will strengthen you and help you; I will uphold you with my righteous right hand.

Isaiah 41:10 (NIV)

Alone in the hospital room, I awaited word from the nurse about how my mother's surgery was going. Her life, as well as ours, was undergoing major change. Before she came home, we would need to build a ramp, move furniture, buy a wheelchair and schedule therapy appointments. She would have to learn to walk again. The list seemed endless, and I felt helpless.

I walked back and forth repeating the words above from Isaiah. Turning to these 'I am' and 'I will' statements from Isaiah reminded me that I could rely on God. I did not need to be anxious about the outcome. I did not have to know how it would all work out. God would give me the strength and help I needed. God's righteous hand would hold us all up.

Though many years have passed since that day, these words often come to me in times of distress. Those repetitions over and over in a hospital room have forever etched on my heart God's truth: 'I am. I will.' God's word is true and powerful. When we study and memorise scripture, it will always be present to help us remember – and then find peace in – God's promise to be present with us, especially in times of crisis.

Prayer: *Dear God, thank you for your strength and your promise to be with us. Amen*

Thought for the day: Even when the Bible isn't in my hand, God's word can be in my heart.

Rebecca Ruth Whisnant (Alabama, USA)

Sisyphus

Sisyphus, a character from Greek mythology, cunningly cheats death twice. As punishment, Zeus condemns him to push a large, heavy rock up a hill. When Sisyphus and his rock reach the top, the rock rolls to the bottom, and Sisyphus must begin his task again – for all eternity. I can only imagine how Sisyphus must have felt each time he stood on the mountaintop, thinking for a moment that maybe this time the rock would stay put. How frustrated and disappointed he must have been as he watched it roll to the bottom yet again!

The story of a man by the pool of Bethesda reminds me of Sisyphus. In Jerusalem, Jesus encounters a man by the pool of Bethesda where people would go in search of healing. The first person to enter the pool after an angel caused the water to move would be healed (see John 5:1–9, KJV). Scripture says that the man 'had been ill for thirty-eight years' and that when Jesus asked him if he wanted to be healed, the man said, 'Sir, I have no one to put me into the pool when the water is stirred up; and while I am making my way, someone else steps down ahead of me' (vv. 5, 7, NRSV). John does not say how long the man had been waiting by the pool, only that 'he had been there a long time' (v. 6).

How exceedingly frustrating it must have been for the man! Each time the water moved he had his chance, only to have someone make it to the water before him. I wonder how many times the man considered giving up. What kept him waiting by the pool? How did he deal with the fear that he might never make it to the water before someone else?

Too often it is easier to imagine that our lives bear more resemblance to Sisyphus than to the man by the pool – easier to imagine that our persistence will never pay off, that we are condemned to struggle forever against the burden of whatever challenge we are facing. What sets the man by the pool apart from the myth is not only the obvious miracle in the text but a second one that I see: the man remained by the pool. Against the odds, knowing he might never enter the water, he remained determined to try. We have the luxury of knowing how his story ends, but I wouldn't fault the man for doubting that things would ever change for him. I can only imagine how easy it would have been for him to lose faith. Knowing that he kept trying makes the story all the more miraculous to me.

Sometimes I feel like Sisyphus, pushing endlessly against stress, uncertainty or exhaustion. When I stand on the mountaintop and watch my rock roll to the bottom, I remind myself of the stories from scripture that give me every reason to believe that things could be different. Jesus, speaking to the man by the pool, said, 'Stand up, take your mat and walk' (v. 8). And that is what happened: 'At once the man... took up his mat and began to walk' (v. 9). Although my life might not change as suddenly and I might not get the miracle I want or expect, I hold on to hope that tomorrow could be better than today. When I am at my lowest point and ready to quit, my faith gives me the strength and fortitude to keep going. And that in itself is often a miracle.

Several meditations in this issue address persistence and moving forward with faith. You may want to read the meditations for 2, 3, 6, 11, 18 and 24 May; 3, 9, 16 and 24 June; 4, 12, 20, 22, 25, 28 and 31 July; 1, 2, 3, 7, 12, 19, 21 and 27 August before responding to the reflection questions below.

QUESTIONS FOR REFLECTION

1 When have you struggled with a task or life event that felt repetitive and futile? What did you learn from this experience?

2 Recall another miracle in scripture in which the character persists against the odds. What are some similarities between this miracle and the one found in John 5:1–9? What are some differences?

3 If you could ask the man whom Jesus healed one question, what would it be?

Andrew Garland Breeden
Acquisitions editor

A tether of love

Read John 10:11–15

'I am the good shepherd. I know my own and my own know me, just as the Father knows me and I know the Father.'
John 10:14–15 (NRSV)

Living on a farm can be a dangerous place for a three-year-old boy. When my mother was working outdoors, she would clip the strap of my overalls to the clothesline so I wouldn't wander off. She showed her love by devising this contraption for my protection. I could jump and run up and down the line and still be safe from the deep waters of the nearby irrigation ditch.

This and similar memories of my childhood always remind me of God's love. Unlike my mother's clothesline tether, God gives us overflowing love by allowing us free will. We can choose to stay close to God or walk in our own direction. At times, we all have chosen our own way and suffered the inevitable consequences. Yet God is still there, loving us back into relationship.

Each of us can step into this day filled with trust in God's promise of protective love. God will never leave us or abandon us, and, if we are willing to listen, God will direct our steps.

Prayer: *Dear God, help us each day to seek and follow the guidance we find in your word. Amen*

Thought for the day: Even when I choose my own way, God still loves me.

John Archer (Florida, USA)

Joy in the present

Read Psalm 139:13–18

Do not say, 'Why were the old days better than these?' For it is not wise to ask such questions.
Ecclesiastes 7:10 (NIV)

I found myself longing for 'the good old days'. My radio was regularly tuned to an oldies station, I watched old rerun episodes on TV and I frequently griped about the large chain stores sprouting up in my neighbourhood. When my usual market was replaced by a chain store, I stopped in to shop. Once inside, I discovered the joys of its increased selection and wider aisles. This pleasant discovery led me to try some different radio and TV stations, only to find I enjoyed many of their programmes as well. Oh, what I had been missing by trying to live in the past!

It's easy to cling to the comfort and familiarity of the past, but in doing so we can lose our enthusiasm for the present and hope for the future. In today's reading, the psalmist assures us that God wrote our days before they existed. God knows our past and present, and God will be by our side in the future. When we avoid moving forward, we may miss the blessings God has in store for us.

Following God's will for me to live fully in the present has expanded my joy and made me a better instrument of God's love. Daily I ask, 'What new experiences can I embrace today?'

Prayer: *Heavenly Father, we trust you with all our days – past, present and future. May we live each day in joyful service to you. Amen*

Thought for the day: 'This is the day that the Lord has made; let us rejoice and be glad in it' (Psalm 118:24, NRSV).

Monica A. Andermann (New York, USA)

Christ is our strength

Read Philippians 4:4–13

I can do all this through him who gives me strength.
Philippians 4:13 (NIV)

My grandfather was the only father figure in our home and the main provider. He owned a butcher shop, and I remember that we always had the best choice of meats for our meals. We always had our uniforms, shoes and supplies for the school year. Though we were not wealthy, we never lacked for anything.

Everything was going well until my grandfather suffered a heart attack and died before we could get him to the hospital. His death was painful for all the family. We had no one to care for us or for the business that we did not know how to manage. Over time, we lost the business because of mounting debt. Where once we enjoyed a comfortable life, we now experienced deprivation.

In one of the Bible studies in which I participated with the church youth group, we studied Paul's letter to the Philippians. Paul, a servant of God, endured much adversity, yet he remained firm in giving thanks and praise to God.

And so, by placing our trust and faith in Christ's strength, our family turned the corner; we survived! We knew that God would provide what we needed and would help us overcome our adversity.

Prayer: *Merciful God, thank you for helping us overcome our troubles and for giving us family and loved ones. We pray in the name of Jesus. Amen*

Thought for the day: My troubles are no match for the strength of Christ.

Ysanny Luciano Guzman (Dominican Republic)

Living proof

Read Psalm 42

Jesus said unto him, Thou shalt love the Lord thy God with all thy heart, and with all thy soul, and with all thy mind. This is the first and great commandment.

Matthew 22:37–38 (KJV)

It only takes a few minutes on social media to notice that many people present a picture of their lives as filled with only happiness and fun. But our relationship with God requires more honesty about our disappointment and pain as well as our joy.

For me, there is no greater disappointment than my disability. Most people would say that I have adapted well to not being able to walk; but inside I am still sad. Through much prayer, the Holy Spirit revealed to me that I had hidden my resentment so deep within my heart that I didn't even realise it was there. Letting God into that dark place meant having to admit that I was angry at God for this happening to me in the first place. Coming to grips with that truth was the key to my healing.

Through the light of God's love, the Holy Spirit gradually changed my perspective. I began to see how blessed I am to be able to walk on crutches! My new mission is to use my body, just as it is, for God's glory.

It's scary to reveal your whole heart to God. But if you take that leap, God can magnify the good and heal the hurt. I promise. I am living proof.

Prayer: *Dear God, help us to love you with our whole heart and to share everything we feel and experience with you. Amen*

Thought for the day: Being honest with God leads to healing and wholeness.

Brian Valdez (Pennsylvania, USA)

Finding beauty in ugly places

Read John 1:1–5

The light shines in the darkness, and the darkness has not overcome it.
John 1:5 (NIV)

I was very fortunate to go on holiday to Botswana. I saw some amazing sights, met some lovely people and watched some incredible animals. My camera clicked all day long!

As we drove along a rough track one morning we suddenly spotted numerous tiny yellow butterflies fluttering all around. There were hundreds of them. It was breathtakingly beautiful. Some landed on the ground before taking to the air again. Our guide explained that they were feeding on the elephant dung on the road, from which they took moisture and salts. Who would have thought that a pile of animal dung, of all places, would give rise to such a dazzling display?

Sometimes it's hard to see beauty in the 'stinky' parts of life. It's hard to see God when times are tough, when we feel there is darkness and evil all around us and when there seems to be no hope. Yet even in the darkest places and through our most troubled experiences the light and beauty of God is there. Keep looking and you too may be dazzled by the glory and grace of God, in the times and places where you would least expect to find him.

Prayer: *Dear Lord, though we may be experiencing a dark and difficult time, may we yet see your glory and grace and find hope and comfort. Amen*

Thought for the day: Where have I seen God's beauty in a time of darkness?

Pam Lewis (England, United Kingdom)

PRAYER FOCUS: THE PEOPLE OF BOTSWANA

Anchor of hope

Read Acts 27:13–26

Fearing that we would be dashed against the rocks, they dropped four anchors from the stern and prayed for daylight.
Acts 27:29 (NIV)

The apostle Paul had been arrested and was sailing to Rome, accompanied by nearly 300 people, when they ended up in a horrible storm. They were helpless and fearful, and disaster was waiting around the corner.

In the middle of their struggles, an angel of the Lord appeared to Paul and promised that all of them would be saved. Those words gave the apostle hope and became an anchor for his soul, even stronger than the anchors of the ship. As we read in Hebrews 6:19, 'We have this hope as an anchor for the soul, firm and secure.'

God is trustworthy in all situations. None of us can avoid storms in life. When we encounter difficulties, we may try to find our anchor in money, good health or a secure job. But we always have an invisible anchor available: Jesus Christ. He went through an unimaginable storm on the cross and rose again to be with us. Let us learn to rest in Christ, the anchor of our souls.

Prayer: *Dear God, thank you for your faithfulness. Help us to trust in the anchor your hope provides as we pray, 'Father, hallowed be your name, your kingdom come. Give us each day our daily bread. Forgive us our sins, for we also forgive everyone who sins against us. And lead us not into temptation.'* Amen*

Thought for the day: What anchor of hope will I offer someone today?

Esa-Pekka Mattila (Finland)

PRAYER FOCUS: SAILORS
*Luke 11:2–4

On the train

Read Psalm 86:8–10

How good and pleasant it is when God's people live together in unity!
Psalm 133:1 (NIV)

The train whistle blew as we headed out of the metro station towards the city. I looked out the window until I could no longer see the platform. Then I opened my Bible and began reading for my 20-minute ride to work.

Many commuters prefer a certain carriage in the train, so it isn't unusual to see the same people every day. After several days, I noticed more and more people reading their Bibles. After a few weeks, our carriage came alive with soft chatter and laughter and discussions about church, sermons and scripture.

One day a young man in traditional Jewish dress boarded the train. He continued to stand even though the seat next to me was empty. The next day he seemed reluctant but sat down beside me and began to scroll through his cell phone. When we stopped, he hurried off the train. On the third day, despite other empty seats, he sat down beside me. I smiled and then went back to my reading. Out of the corner of my eye I saw him pull out his cell phone, and as he slowly scrolled he began praying out loud in Hebrew. Since then, he has sat beside me every day. He prays out loud while I read my Bible.

As Christians, we are called to be witnesses of Christ's love for the world. In just a short month our train carriage had transformed from a sombre space into a vibrant place of worship.

Prayer: *God of Abraham, as we go about our daily routines, help us to remember that you can use any situation to show your love for others. Amen*

Thought for the day: My daily actions can invite others into worship.

Susan Cosper (Maryland, USA)

PRAYER FOCUS: INTERFAITH COMMUNITIES

Thinking ahead

Read 2 Peter 1:3–9

*Forgetting what is behind and straining towards what is ahead,
I press on towards the goal to win the prize for which God has called
me heavenwards in Christ Jesus.*
Philippians 3:13–14 (NIV)

A little girl had just returned home after visiting an elderly lady with her mother. 'Mummy,' she said, 'when I am an old lady I want to be like that lovely lady.' 'In that case,' replied her mother, 'you'd better start practising now because it takes a very long time.'

What are we aiming for in life? What kind of people do we hope to become? Our answer to those questions affects our thinking, our attitude, our speech and our actions, and determines the way we develop as Christians.

When we read 2 Peter 1:3–9, we find that the way to develop Christian character is a step by step process, starting from the time we come to Christ right through to the end of our life. As we learn of Jesus in God's word, listen to him as we pray and obey him, he continues to gradually change us. It doesn't happen automatically; it needs serious commitment from us and we shouldn't expect it to be easy.

Do we want to be like Jesus? Then we must start practising now, because it is a lifetime's work. Young or old, new believer or long-time Christian, let us, as the apostle Paul wrote, press on right to the end of our life's journey towards that goal.

Prayer: *Help us, Lord, today and every day, to keep our aim before us, so that we may keep growing to be more like Jesus. Amen*

Thought for the day: I will give my utmost for his highest.

Hazel V. Thompson (England, United Kingdom)

Which path?

Read Psalm 119:1–8

Direct me in the paths of your commands, for there I find delight.
Psalm 119:35 (NIV)

We consulted maps and considered terrain and distance before our group of ten family members embarked on a moderate hike to a mountain lookout. A few metres from the trailhead the path branched off in different directions. We turned left. The hike became more and more difficult. None of the expected trail markers appeared. We reasoned that the wide path did not need markers, so we kept climbing. At the top of a long climb the path branched again with no markers. Our rising doubts peaked. Did we take the correct path? Two people went ahead to survey the area and discovered that the path to our right matched our expectations with a gentle climb and level areas.

We had chosen the wrong path, which had led us to a challenging and potentially dangerous climb. But when we changed course, we returned to the correct path.

In today's scripture reading, the psalmist uses God's law, words and instructions as a road map to life. Repeatedly the psalmist writes of how God guides his steps and makes his path level. Without God's law my steps slip and my days become a struggle. Thankfully, we are not doomed to the wrong path forever. God makes a way for us to return to the path that leads us where God would have us go.

Prayer: *Dear God, give us wisdom each day to follow your way. Amen*

Thought for the day: With God's guidance I can always find my way.

Lorilee Guenter (Saskatchewan, Canada)

PRAYER FOCUS: SOMEONE ON A DANGEROUS PATH

Crumbling empires

Read Matthew 6:19–24

The Lord proclaims: Cursed are those who trust in mere humans, who depend on human strength and turn their hearts from the Lord… Happy are those who trust in the Lord, who rely on the Lord.
Jeremiah 17:5, 7 (CEB)

Standing in the marketplace of ancient Megiddo in Israel, I closed my eyes and imagined the swirl of activity occurring on this spot 3,000 years earlier. Once considered the jewel of northern Israel, the location hosted Solomon's stables and Ahab's winter palace. Merchants would have been hawking their wares, politicians debating hot topics, children playing among the booths. I opened my eyes to scan the ruins of what had been a great cultural centre. I surveyed the crumbling pillars and piles of rock, awestruck by the contrast of then and now. The greatest treasures earth offers will someday crumble, including any 'empires' I attempt to build.

In today's quoted scripture, the prophet declares that relying on the flesh results in disaster. When we seek security in our wealth, career or intelligence, we will fail. However, trusting in God promises an enriching life of blessing, delivering us from misguided dependence on current culture. Nothing our world offers will last – not power, prosperity or popularity. Everything, everyone, is destined to wither and fade. When we look to this world for fulfilment, we live with uncertainty; but we can always rely on God. Knowing and loving God by loving others – these things will continue through eternity and never crumble.

Prayer: *Dear God, empower us to focus our hearts on you, not on the crumbling empires around us. Amen*

Thought for the day: Trusting in God brings security that the world can never give.

Barney Cargile III (California, USA)

Distractions

Read Matthew 14:13–23

When he sent them away, he went up onto a mountain by himself to pray. Evening came and he was alone.
Matthew 14:23 (CEB)

I once tried making bread. It had just four ingredients: flour, water, salt and yeast. I thought, 'How hard could it be?' I mixed the ingredients to form a sticky dough, covered it with a damp cloth and plastic bag, and set it by the stove to rise for an hour. I got distracted, and before I knew it, 90 minutes had passed. The yeast had multiplied so much that the dough had overrun its bowl. I moved it to the oven anyway, and I ended up with a loaf that was golden on the outside – but hollow in the middle.

My distractedness caused my dough to rise too much that day. Distraction also sometimes negatively affects my spiritual life. As a parent who works full-time, I can get so caught up in life's everyday demands – demands of my job, staying on top of my email inbox or planning loads of laundry around who has the fewest clean socks – that my soul feels as hollow as that bread. When I prioritise reading scripture, praying and spending time with God in solitude, I make room in my life to better serve the kingdom of heaven.

Prayer: *Dear Lord, help us to care for ourselves as we also care for others. Nurture our faith so that your love and mercy can rise within us. Amen*

Thought for the day: How will I prioritise my faith today?

Stacey Elza (West Virginia, USA)

Comfort for others

Read 2 Corinthians 1:3–7

Praise be to the God and Father of our Lord Jesus Christ, the Father of compassion and the God of all comfort, who comforts us in all our troubles, so that we can comfort those in any trouble with the comfort we ourselves receive from God.
2 Corinthians 1:3–4 (NIV)

I had just finished high school when my father died. I felt my world collapsing as I stood by his body and reflected on all the promises he had made to me: to care for me and support my education to any level I desired.

I cried and could not be consoled. But then I felt as if God whispered to me, 'Your father is dead, but your heavenly Father is alive and will see you through.' Those words sank deep into my heart and strengthened me. I have since gone to university and finished my first and second degrees with the help of God.

The comfort God gave me enables me to console others going through the same pain. In the years since my father died, I've had many friends who have lost loved ones and felt overwhelmed with grief. But each time I shared the soothing words that God gave me and how God saw me through my greatest ordeal.

God does not abandon us in hard times, and our experiences can help us bless others. We can take solace in God in difficult times and find the courage to help others who suffer the same. Whatever pain we feel today, God's comfort will sustain us and help us care for others.

Prayer: *Dear Lord, help us to understand how the comfort you give us in trouble can console others in despair. Amen*

Thought for the day: I will share the comfort God has given me with others today.

Olaiya Muyiwa Benralph (Federal Capital Territory, Nigeria)

A small thing

Read Matthew 10:29–31
'Even the very hairs of your head are all numbered.'
Matthew 10:30 (NIV)

I heard a beautiful song on the radio years ago that I immediately loved. I only heard it once, but it has stuck with me. Many times since I heard it, I've wished I knew its name so I could buy it and listen to it often. I even spent an hour or two searching the internet for what I thought were key phrases from the song – all to no avail.

This morning on my daily walk, I was listening to a music streaming service, which allows you to choose a song or artist that you like, then also plays similar songs. As one of my favourite songs was playing, a fleeting thought of that nameless song entered my mind. Then about 15 minutes later, the song for which I had been searching almost five years started playing! It was a very small thing, but in that moment I felt God's presence and was reminded how much God cares about us and about what we care about, however small it may be.

At times I have felt utterly alone, as if God had completely forgotten me. And then something like this happens, which reminds me in a tangible way of how personal God is. And God is not just our heavenly Father; God is our friend too. It's little moments like this that remind me that my friend, my Father God, is so very faithful, loving and trustworthy.

Prayer: *Father God, help us to remember just how much you love and care about us. Help us to notice your mighty, merciful hand in the midst of daily life. Amen*

Thought for the day: Ordinary moments can be the best reminders of God's presence.

Anna R. Johnson (Virginia, USA)

PRAYER FOCUS: GRATITUDE FOR GOD'S PRESENCE

Patient in prayer

Read 1 Thessalonians 5:16–24
The prayer of the righteous is powerful and effective.
James 5:16 (NRSV)

When I was young, we lived 2,000 miles from my paternal grandparents. I was able to see them only a couple of times in their lifetimes. They had little money, but every year my grandmother sent me a small present for Christmas and my birthday.

The 'worst' present she ever sent me was a cloth bookmark with a tassel on the bottom. It had an embroidered picture of Jesus wearing a crown of thorns, along with stylised flowers and the words 'May heaven's blessings be with you.' For some reason I kept it, even though my parents and I were not Christians.

I found out later that my grandmother had prayed for me every day of my life until she died. That made the bookmark one of my prized possessions. What patience, love and strong faith she had, to pray every day for a little boy thousands of miles away whom she hardly ever saw.

I believe it was her prayers and those of my grandfather that brought me to Christ. And her example convinced me of the value of patient prayer. It is easy to get tired of praying for a particular person or situation, and sometimes it doesn't seem to do any good. But God hears and will always answer with divine wisdom.

Prayer: *Thank you, Lord, for those who faithfully and patiently pray for us. Grant us patience to pray persistently for others. Amen*

Thought for the day: It may take time, but God will answer my prayers.

Ken Claar (Idaho, USA)

Give the best

Read Hebrews 11:1–6

Without faith it is impossible to please God, because anyone who comes to him must believe that he exists and that he rewards those who earnestly seek him.
Hebrews 11:6 (NIV)

When I was interviewed by someone from a TV channel after resigning from my job, a reporter asked me if I felt a sense of loss at leaving my position in a prestigious company and giving up a large income to be a mother. I replied, 'Not at all! In fact, I'm grateful to be a mother so that I can teach my children to love God and others, to glorify God and to give their best to God whatever their profession in the future.'

The examples of Abel and Enoch in today's reading encourage me to give my best – whatever my profession – and to live in a way that pleases God. God is pleased by those who earnestly seek to trust, give their best and live in obedience to God. We are called to follow God even when, according to the world, we are giving up something good in order to do it. But God always wants what is best for us and will lead us to what is good.

Prayer: *Loving God, thank you for all the opportunities you put before us. Give us the courage to follow where you lead. Amen*

Thought for the day: God wants what is best for me.

Linda Chandra (Banten, Indonesia)

Lost and found

Read Luke 15:3–7

I have strayed like a lost sheep. Seek your servant, for I have not forgotten your commands.
Psalm 119:176 (NIV)

A few years ago, my grandparents' dog, Lady, went missing. They looked everywhere for her, from the fields to the forest to the town and even to the town down the road.

A week later, Lady was still missing; we had almost lost hope. My dad went out for one final search of the countryside. After about an hour he came back. As he opened the front door, Lady appeared and ran straight for my grandparents. Everyone rejoiced, happy that Lady had been found.

Sometimes we get lost in the distractions of the world around us. We have more to do than we have time for. School, work, taking care of children, taking care of parents, extracurricular activities and much more fill our time. We may almost seem to lose track of ourselves. However, when we recount the story from Luke, we find comfort knowing God is searching for us just as the shepherd searched for the one sheep that had wandered away. When we slow our lives down enough to focus on God's presence, we find a celebration of a renewed life – ours!

Through our experience with Lady, I have renewed faith that God searches, finds and brings us back with joyous celebration. Just as we did for Lady. Just as the shepherd does for the sheep.

Prayer: *Loving God, when we feel lost and troubled, remind us that you are always nearby, ready to guide us back home to you. Amen*

Thought for the day: No matter how lost I feel, God will always find me.

Josey McChesney (Missouri, USA)

Gratitude

Read Isaiah 41:8–14

Do not be anxious about anything, but in every situation, by prayer and petition, with thanksgiving, present your requests to God.
Philippians 4:6 (NIV)

I'm terrified of drowning, so I've avoided water most of my life. Before I turned 40, however, I decided to face my fears and take swimming lessons. My coach knew I was nervous and had me do an exercise each week before he started his instruction. I gripped the side of the pool and bobbed up and down, dunking my head under water and coming back up for air. I did this 100 times before the fear left my body. Then I was relaxed enough to learn.

God knows that we are prone to worry. Scripture repeatedly tells us not to be afraid, not to fear, not to be anxious. Besides wanting better for us than a life of fear, like my wise swim coach God knows we cannot receive instruction if worried thoughts distract us. So God gives us an exercise to help: pray about every situation with thanksgiving.

Anxious thoughts and gratitude cannot occupy our minds at the same time. When troubles increase, we may find it difficult to name even one reason to be thankful. But we can start by saying, 'Thank you, God, for allowing me to come to you with my requests.' God will take our prayer of thanksgiving and help us to give thanks in all circumstances.

Prayer: *Dear God, thank you for your promise to strengthen us and help us. Open our eyes to your many blessings. We want to have thankful hearts. Amen*

Thought for the day: Rather than focusing on my fears, I can focus on giving thanks.

Amy Lynn Taylor (Colorado, USA)

PRAYER FOCUS: FOR RELIEF FROM WORRY

God never forsakes us

Read 1 Kings 8:54–61

'May the Lord our God be with us as he was with our ancestors; may he never leave us nor forsake us.'
1 Kings 8:57 (NIV)

In 2001, a family in our neighbourhood suffered a terrible loss. One day a fire broke out in their house. Nobody was at home, but the house was completely destroyed. All the family had left were the clothes they had worn that day. They had no savings, and the house was not insured.

After the fire, the family started to receive help from members of the church where the father served as a pastor. One woman offered her apartment for the family to live in free of charge. Friends started to raise funds for construction of a new house. God blessed and provided the necessary means at every stage of the process, and now the family has a new home.

I have seen God's grace at work in the middle of disaster. God never forsakes us, and God prompts us to open our hearts and help those in trouble. The apostle Paul reminds us in Philippians 4:14, 'It was good of you to share in my troubles.' The experience of my neighbours taught me how important it is to remember our brothers and sisters in hard times. Let us do our best to love and support one another.

Prayer: *Dear God of grace, we thank you for your great love, mercy and help in all our hardships. May your name be blessed. Amen*

Thought for the day: No matter what, God will never forsake me.

Oleg Tservonoi (Tallinn, Estonia)

Beyond the galaxies

Read Ephesians 3:14–21

When I look at your heavens, the work of your fingers, the moon and the stars that you have established; what are human beings that you are mindful of them, mortals that you care for them?
Psalm 8:3–4 (NRSV)

Have you ever gazed at the endless expanse of stars and felt small? It is hard to grasp the size of our own solar system, much less the Milky Way galaxy. Scientists estimate the existence of two trillion galaxies in the observable universe. The mind-boggling size of the universe can leave individuals feeling quite insignificant, especially when we remember that our God simply spoke everything into existence (see Genesis 1).

When we try to comprehend the size of our physical universe, we realise that we are less than a speck of dust compared to the vastness of creation. It seems that we should be easily lost or forgotten. I ponder as the psalmist did, 'What are human beings that you are mindful of them?' Why would God make the universe so big? Why would God care about us compared to all of creation? Perhaps God designed the vast expanse of creation to illustrate the magnitude – the 'breadth and length and height and depth' – of God's love for us (see Ephesians 3:18). For if the same God who spoke it all into existence would send his own Son to die on our behalf, that love must extend beyond creation itself. And that is truly mind-boggling!

Prayer: *Dear God, help us to understand the breadth of your love for us so that we can learn to love you and your creation better. Amen*

Thought for the day: Despite the vastness of the universe, God's love for me is greater still.

Trudy Chun (Texas, USA)

Always joyful

Read Psalm 23

If we live, we live to the Lord, and if we die, we die to the Lord; so then, whether we live or whether we die, we are the Lord's.
Romans 14:8 (NRSV)

I am originally from Gujarat, India. One of my greatest blessings is that all my children received good educations and now have settled in Australia and the United States. I have been interested in mission work since I was a child, and now I have been able to share the gospel in various cities in Australia and the US.

For a time I returned to Gujarat to serve the Lord by helping those in need. While I was there, doctors found tumours in two places in my brain. At the same time, I was suffering from severe problems with diabetes. The doctors warned me that I had a short time to live. But I was not afraid of this news because I believe death will take me to the joyful presence of the Lord. My doctors were surprised by my joyful attitude. In spite of this serious health condition, I have been joyfully involved in serving the Lord by helping people in need. I do not worry about my health. I am more concerned about serving the Lord than I am afraid of death. It gives me great joy to be involved in the Lord's service.

Prayer: *O Father, accept the ways we help others in service to you. By our example, allow others to find it in their hearts to serve you as well. Amen*

Thought for the day: Being able to live my life in service to God brings me joy.

Ishwarbhai Hirabhai Dabhi (New Jersey, USA)

Bringing out the best

Read Matthew 5:13–16

'You are the salt of the earth; but if salt has lost its taste, how can its saltiness be restored? It is no longer good for anything, but is thrown out and trampled under foot.'
Matthew 5:13 (NRSV)

As I was quickly making lunch, the delicious scent of pumpkin soup filled my nose. I had added chicken, seasonings and some vegetables. But when I uncovered the pot and took a taste, I gagged. In my rush, I had forgotten the salt.

As I carefully measured and added two teaspoons of sea salt, I could not help but wonder, 'What is it about these small, white crystals?' Without salt, even the best meal may not turn out right. Salt dissolves and brings out the best in the ingredients around it.

I think this function of salt represents what God has called the church to be: a people who influence and add to those around them for the better. What a shame if in the busyness of life I should forget to be salt. As just one grain, I can do only so much; but together, as siblings in Christ, we add to and transform the flavour of life all around the world.

Prayer: *Dear Lord, help us to be salt wherever we go. May your presence in us influence and improve the world around us. Amen*

Thought for the day: I can use my faith to bring out the best in others.

Amorelle Browne (Grenada)

PRAYER FOCUS: COOKS

Shifting shadows

Read Psalm 27:1–5

Every good and perfect gift is from above, coming down from the Father of the heavenly lights, who does not change like shifting shadows.
James 1:17 (NIV)

The warmth of the sun lured me to the window. I noticed long shadows stretching across the snow-covered ground from barren trees blocking the light. A breeze rustled the branches and shifted the patches of darkness. As I observed the contrast, it dawned on me that shadows only occur in the presence of light. I may feel overshadowed by darkness, but the light is still there.

I was reminded of how my diagnosis of ovarian cancer cast shadows of doubt, fear and anxiety across my horizon. I had more questions than answers: Would I survive? What side effects of chemotherapy would I experience? What about my future?

Amid my surgery and chemotherapy, slivers of light pierced the darkness. I recalled God's goodness and faithfulness in the past, and truths from God's word shined the light of hope, faith and peace into my heart.

The circumstances of my life had changed, but God never changes. God is the light that shines in darkness. Even though I encountered shadows in that season, they were fleeting. God's light penetrated the darkness and offered me the hope and courage I needed to face my challenges.

Prayer: *God of light, when we are overwhelmed by fear and anxiety, help us to remember your love. Amen*

Thought for the day: Even when I feel overcome by shadows, I can find slivers of God's light.

Joanie Shawhan (Wisconsin, USA)

Intentional farmers

Read Matthew 13:1–8, 18–23

'As for what was sown on good soil, this is the one who hears the word and understands it, who indeed bears fruit and yields, in one case a hundredfold, in another sixty, and in another thirty.'
Matthew 13:23 (NRSV)

When I read today's parable, I find myself wondering, 'How can I spread the seeds of faith everywhere I go?' We can spread the seeds of faith on any soil and leave the rest to God, but having grown up in a farming community I can't help but think of farmers when I read the parable. Every farmer I know prepares the soil, clears out rocks and weeds, and lays down fertiliser before planting seeds. The farmer then tends the crops to give them the best chance of thriving.

Thinking about planting from this perspective reminds me that while it is important to share my faith widely, I should not be disheartened if some seeds do not take root. I can leave those to God and focus on nurturing the budding faith of those ready for a deeper relationship with God. Jesus spread his message everywhere he went and excluded no one. But like a farmer preparing land for planting, Jesus also invested much time in the first disciples and those closest to him.

The parable of the sower invites us to consider how we are planting seeds of faith each day. And the example of the careful farmer invites us to go further: How am I investing in specific people and helping them to grow in faith? We can follow Jesus' example and share our faith with the wider world but also take time to nurture the faith of those around us.

Prayer: *Dear Lord, help us to be intentional in the way we use our gifts to share our faith with others. Amen*

Thought for the day: How will I be intentional in the way I spread the gospel?

Paul Cillo (Pennsylvania, USA)

The power of solitude

Read Mark 1:35–38

Jesus often withdrew to lonely places and prayed.
Luke 5:16 (NIV)

Most humans yearn for group interaction, so it can be considered odd to delight in solitude. But the 'odd' people stand out. They break away from the herd by doing something different.

Many of us desire to always be part of some conversation or part of the collective in some way. We can't stand to be alone. We may not know what to do with ourselves, or we just have FOMO (fear of missing out). Maybe we are afraid of being alone with our thoughts. But why should we fear being alone?

Jesus regularly withdrew from his disciples to pray and be alone with God. If even Jesus, who was the Son of God, found it necessary to have periods of solitude, how much more do we need it with all the digital noise constantly around us?

Following Jesus' example by making time to be alone to think or pray or simply be still can re-energise us and help us to live life fully.

Prayer: *Dear God, help us to find periods of solitude and to use that time to grow nearer to you. We pray as Jesus taught us, 'Our Father which art in heaven, Hallowed be thy name. Thy kingdom come. Thy will be done, as in heaven, so in earth. Give us day by day our daily bread. And forgive us our sins; for we also forgive every one that is indebted to us. And lead us not into temptation; but deliver us from evil.'* Amen*

Thought for the day: Solitude can re-energise my faith.

Thando Meck (Harare, Zimbabwe)

My story isn't over

Read 1 Kings 19:1–9

*'Do not fear, for I am with you; do not be dismayed, for I am your God.
I will strengthen you and help you; I will uphold you with my righteous
right hand.'*
Isaiah 41:10 (NIV)

It was too hard. I had tried everything, and nothing was working. I was
stuck, and nothing was going to change. I was at work, so I excused
myself from the office and found a quiet room alone. As I sat curled
up against the cold wall, I closed my eyes and prayed that God would
take my life.

My mental health had been deteriorating for months. I was getting
help, but if life was going to be like this, I didn't think I wanted to live it.
Thankfully, God's plans were different from my own.

As I was reading the Bible, God reminded me of Elijah. We often
remember Elijah as incredibly strong. Yet, Elijah was human, and he
cried the same prayer I did: 'I have had enough, Lord… Take my life'
(1 Kings 19:4, NIV).

In response to Elijah's prayer, God sent him sustenance for the next
part of his journey. His story wasn't over yet. Neither is mine, and neither
is yours. When we feel like we don't have strength, or we feel like we
have nothing more to give, God beckons us to keep going. We are never
alone; God walks with us every step of the way.

Prayer: *Dear Lord, you know what is best for us. Thank you for giving
us strength for the day, even when we feel that we have nothing left to
give. Amen*

Thought for the day: I will seek God's strength in my times of need.

Tina Clark (Massachusetts, USA)

Steep hills

Read Isaiah 40:28–31

My grace is sufficient for thee: for my strength is made perfect in weakness.
2 Corinthians 12:9 (KJV)

Growing old is for the birds, they say, and I would most wholeheartedly agree! But I sure wouldn't trade the wisdom that has come with age for my younger years. So in these latter years of graying hair, one morning my husband and I decided it would be good to begin walking for exercise. Each day we start by going down our street, then turning the corner to a nice long, flat stretch. But to make it back home, we have to climb a steep hill. That's when I say to my husband, 'I'd like to grab your arm to help me up!'

Our morning walk has become a great time for us to pray once we come to that hill – I just can't talk and walk it at the same time. It seems to be God's way of giving us a perfect time to be still – a perfect prayer time.

I've come across some 'steep hills' in life that make me feel pretty weak. That's when I grab hold of the promise that God's strength is made perfect in our weakness. Actually, I try to remember to rely on God every day – not just when steep hills confront me. But when they do, God's grace and strength prove sufficient every time.

Prayer: *Dear Lord, strengthen our faith. Help us to remember that your strength never wavers and that you are ready to help us when we call out to you. Amen*

Thought for the day: No hill is too steep when God walks with me.

Dara H. Gunnell (North Carolina, USA)

PRAYER FOCUS: SOMEONE BEGINNING A NEW PRAYER PRACTICE

The royal law

Read Mark 12:28–34

If you really keep the royal law found in Scripture, 'Love your neighbour as yourself', you are doing right.
James 2:8 (NIV)

Not long after we got married, my wife and I went to a sandwich shop. We were about to eat when a man in ragged clothes gazed at us and asked for food. At first, I tried to pretend that I didn't notice him, but my wife looked at him. She gave her sandwich to that man. I pouted and thought, 'How impractical! It is easier to get rid of this beggar by giving him a few coins than buying him such costly food.'

After we went home, I pondered the incident. I felt ashamed of my attitude towards that man. I had been selfish. I thought about my many blessings. Those blessings are God's grace – not my own achievements. And God wants me to share those blessings with everyone.

When I had the opportunity to share at least one of those blessings, I wanted to share only the leftover part by giving the man a few coins. I failed to practice the royal law of love in today's quoted verse. Because I gave more importance to my pleasure than his need, I was not loving him 'as myself'. God has shown us how to love our neighbours as ourselves through Jesus, who not only taught us the royal law of love but lived it out by giving up his life on the cross.

Prayer: *Dear Lord, fill our hearts with compassion so that we can love others as ourselves. Amen*

Thought for the day: How will I love someone as myself today?

Hitesh J. Solanki (Gujarat, India)

Don't look back

Read Genesis 19:15–26

Lot's wife looked back, and she became a pillar of salt.
Genesis 19:26 (NIV)

I remember the first time I heard my dad read the story of Lot's wife. As a child, I didn't understand why Lot's wife looked back. I wanted to yell, 'Don't look back!' But she did, and her life ended. Now, as an adult, I understand why she might have looked back. She was leaving the familiar. She may have loved someone she left behind or even the town itself.

At times in my life, I've had a hard time moving forward without grieving over what I've left behind. When we moved to a different state, far away from family, it was hard to leave the familiar and those I loved. I ended up making a list of the reasons we moved. When I struggled with letting go of the past, I would read the list and remember God's direction.

We can trust God when God says it's time to move forward and not look back. One consequence for looking back is that moving forward becomes more difficult than it needs to be. Our fate may not be as drastic as Lot's wife, but no doubt we suffer when we disobey God's call to move forward and refuse to leave the past behind.

So when God says to go, we can follow in confidence, knowing that God will lead us to the best place for our growth and joy.

Prayer: *Father God, help us to look forward to what you are doing in our lives and never to look back in regret. Amen*

Thought for the day: With God I can go forward confidently.

Melinda Eye Cooper (Tennessee, USA)

God's voice

Read John 10:22–30

'My sheep listen to my voice; I know them, and they follow me.'
John 10:27 (NIV)

'I can't hear you! Speak louder!' These requests, directed to my wife, were becoming more frequent. Eventually, I had to admit that I was hard of hearing. Hearing aids have helped, but in social settings I struggle to distinguish the voice of the person in front of me from others in the room. Fortunately, my hearing aids are equipped with a setting that allows me to tune out the surrounding sounds so I can focus on the person I want to hear.

Similarly, the noise of voices both internal and external that vie for our attention can distract us from hearing God's voice. It is easy to rush through our Bible reading without taking the time to still our restlessness and ponder the truth of the message. Despite the voices that compete for our attention, if we quiet ourselves and listen, we will hear God speaking.

Today's quoted verse reminds us to listen to Jesus, who is the good shepherd. Jesus knows and loves us and wants us to hear what he has to say. Are we listening? When we step back from the noise and activity of our busy lives, we can listen humbly and quietly for God's guidance.

Prayer: *Dear Lord, you are the shepherd of our lives. Help us to find quiet in our lives so that we can better listen for your voice. Amen*

Thought for the day: Today I will listen for God's voice.

Wayne Greenawalt (Illinois, USA)

PRAYER FOCUS: THOSE WITH HEARING LOSS

Close to home

Read 1 Peter 4:7–11

Each of you should use whatever gift you have received to serve others.

1 Peter 4:10 (NIV)

When I was eight years old, I told God that I wanted to be a missionary. I thought this type of service was the only way to show God my full commitment. As I grew older, I tried to pursue my dream of mission service; but the doors always closed. I didn't understand why God wouldn't use me.

Eventually, God led me to the role of wife, mum and small-business owner. It wasn't what I expected, and at times I felt disillusioned. But what God began to show me was that my call was to be faithful in using what God had entrusted me with. God's plan for me was not full-time mission work in a far country; it was here in my ordinary life that God wanted me to serve.

Whatever our vocation, we have people around us who need God's love. God may call us to be servants right where we are. When a neighbour is going through a hard time, a card, a visit or a home-cooked meal could be the answer to God's call. Similarly, if an elderly acquaintance needs a ride to the doctor's office we can be ready. When we become the hands and feet of Christ to those in our sphere of influence, we are indeed missionaries!

Prayer: *Heavenly Father, we want to serve you now. Show us the opportunities you have already put in front of us right where we are. Amen*

Thought for the day: God will present opportunities for me to serve every day.

Naomi Fata (New York, USA)

A caregiver's testimony

Read 2 Corinthians 4:6–10

'Surely God is my salvation; I will trust and not be afraid. The Lord, the Lord himself, is my strength and my defence.'
Isaiah 12:2 (NIV)

My husband and I have been married for more than 55 years. For the last nine years I have been my husband's full-time caregiver. He depends on me for his every need because he lives with both Alzheimer's and Parkinson's disease. At the end of each day I am exhausted but not shattered.

My family and friends are my support system. They remain in contact with us by visiting or calling. They sustain us with their prayers and words of encouragement. I am grateful, and I thank God for each one of them.

I find my greatest source of comfort and strength in God's word referenced in Isaiah 41:10: 'Do not fear, for I am with you; do not be dismayed, for I am your God. I will strengthen you and help you; I will uphold you with my righteous right hand.' Because God renews my strength each day, I fully trust that no matter how challenging the circumstances, I will not face the new day alone. Thanks be to God.

Prayer: *Loving God, we look to you each day for your unfailing strength, love and grace. In all circumstances, your presence is our blessing, your strength our salvation. Thank you, Lord. Amen*

Thought for the day: God's strength will see me through.

Digna Lebrón Silva (Puerto Rico)

PRAYER FOCUS: CAREGIVERS

The complete regimen

Read James 2:14–24

Just as the body without the spirit is dead, so faith without works is also dead.

James 2:26 (NRSV)

My doctor suggested that I lose weight, and he gave me a new diet plan which I began to follow. However, despite my efforts I was losing very little weight. At my next appointment, I asked my doctor what I was doing wrong. He asked me what exercise I was doing, and for how long. I told him that exercising was too time-consuming and that I figured the right diet should be enough. But he told me it takes exercise to make any diet complete – one without the other will not lead to success.

Sure enough, when I did start mixing the two together daily, I was able to lose weight. And even though I didn't think I had the time for it, after a while exercise began to fit easily into my schedule.

When I first came to the Lord, I learned a similar lesson. In the beginning, daily Bible reading and prayer made me feel better about myself, but I didn't really feel God's Spirit until I began doing volunteer work, both for my church and in my community. That work made the message of Jesus come alive in me. Like my physical body, my spiritual body needs exercise to keep it healthy. Whatever time it takes from my schedule, the reward is always worth the effort.

Prayer: *Heavenly Father, help us to care for our bodies and our spirits so that we may live abundantly with you. Amen*

Thought for the day: Putting my faith into action is my daily work.

Mark A. Carter (Oregon, USA)

Worth the wait

Read Galatians 6:7–10

Let us not become weary in doing good, for at the proper time we will reap a harvest if we do not give up.
Galatians 6:9 (NIV)

When I became a homeowner, I found mowing the lawn stressful. Getting my mower started was a feat in itself, not to mention the hour and a half it took to get the job done. As I've grown accustomed to mowing, however, I've actually begun to enjoy it. I find satisfaction in seeing weeds disappear as I work, and I love to admire the beauty of my lawn when I've finished.

This experience has caused me to wish that more of life was this way. In most of my other efforts, I don't see immediate results the way I do when mowing my lawn: the friend who seemed excited to come to church with me once doesn't come again; after I have taught them for months, my students still make the same mistakes they made before; temptations I thought I had conquered get the best of me yet again.

Today's quoted verse reminds us not to give up on our efforts to do good. We may see the results of our efforts in this life, but not always. God's timetable is different from ours. And even when we may not see it, God is working to mould us into the image of Christ. God promises that if we don't give up, we are sure to reap a harvest worth the wait.

Prayer: *Dear Lord, help us to persevere in our efforts to do good. Amen*

Thought for the day: Even when I do not see results, God is at work in my life.

Jody Williams (Illinois, USA)

Standing firm

Read Romans 1:8–17

'As for me and my household, we will serve the Lord.'
Joshua 24:15 (NIV)

I was raised in a Christian family in Ukraine. Unfortunately my family and other Christians suffered under Soviet rule. As Christian children, we were persecuted in school. We studied hard but always received lower grades than others. When students began to be recruited for an atheist youth organisation, eight of us from Christian families refused to join. As a result we were locked in a classroom for several hours. A teacher yelled at us and ordered us to sign applications, but we did not bend.

After graduation, I wanted to attend university and passed the entrance exams twice. Because of my faith, my name was deleted from the admissions list both times. Despite our persecution, the examples of our parents and grandparents gave us the courage to stand firm in our faith, and they never ceased to pray for us.

Years later when things had changed in our country, my sister and I were walking in town and met the teacher who had humiliated us the most. We were astonished when he said, 'Please forgive me, if you can! I always admired your strong faith but was too afraid to take your side.' I understood then that our lives had given witness to God's mercy and protection. God's power made us strong and enabled us to face our trials.

Prayer: *Dear God, thank you for never forsaking your children, even in the most difficult situations. Amen*

Thought for the day: God's strength and power help me to live faithfully.

Mariya Lohinova (Ukraine)

A big little prayer

Read Proverbs 3:1–6

Trust in the Lord with all your heart and lean not on your own understanding; in all your ways submit to him, and he will make your paths straight.
Proverbs 3:5–6 (NIV)

When I was five or six years old, my granddaddy said, 'I'm going to teach you a big little prayer and this is it: "Help me, Lord."' I remember asking to hear the rest of the prayer, and Granddaddy said that was all of it. He told me that if ever I am in danger, have a problem, am afraid or have to make a decision, I can call on the Lord.

I did not understand then how a prayer could be both big and little, but I believed Granddaddy knew everything so I knew it must have been true. I have always kept that big little prayer close to my heart, and it has served me well many times. I am thankful for this seed of faith that my granddaddy sowed in my life when I was a child. In recent years I began to share this prayer with members of the Bible studies and Sunday school classes that I teach.

When I recite this little prayer, I am trusting God to provide me with God's understanding, just as Proverbs 3:5–6 instructs. God is faithful and will guide our thoughts, words and deeds. We can always call out, 'Help me, Lord.'

Prayer: *Thank you, Lord, for always being with us, guiding and protecting us. Amen*

Thought for the day: Small prayers can create strong connections to God.

Matthew L. Harper (Georgia, USA)

Imitators

Read Ephesians 5:1–2

Do not conform to the pattern of this world, but be transformed by the renewing of your mind. Then you will be able to test and approve what God's will is – his good, pleasing and perfect will.
Romans 12:2 (NIV)

The alarm of a nearby water system woke me up. After several minutes, I heard a mockingbird copying the beeping sound. I smiled at the bird who was copying not another bird's song but a noise from a machine made by humans.

Then I thought about what I copy. How often do I, as a child of God, imitate humanity's way rather than God's way? My amusement faded as I realised that just that week, I had imitated the habits of the world more than once. I was quick to judge a woman's character based on her clothing. I held a conversation questioning the motives behind someone's acts of service. My TV shows, reading and music that week had not portrayed godly values.

In today's reading, Paul encourages us to imitate God's love. But too often, rather than looking on others with the kind of love God shows me, I think and act out of habits and judgements that I have learned from the world around me.

Maybe that is why Paul says that we should follow Christ's example of a life filled with sacrificial love. As we seek to imitate Christ, God can transform our attitudes so that we can grow and act in ways that match God's will for us.

Prayer: *Heavenly Father, thank you for the example of Christ's sacrificial love. Help us to imitate his love in our attitudes and actions. Amen*

Thought for the day: Today I will seek to imitate the love of Christ.

Montra C. Weaver (Texas, USA)

Enough

Read John 6:1–14

When they had all had enough to eat, he said to his disciples, 'Gather the pieces that are left over. Let nothing be wasted.'
John 6:12 (NIV)

I recently participated in a workshop on listening to God. During the session, we were led in an exercise where we were invited to imagine ourselves as part of the feeding of the 5,000. As I immersed myself in the events, I became part of the crowd. I was at the back being jostled by those who wanted a better view of Jesus as he preached. He spoke well, but I had my eye on the food! I was hungry after a long day. I sensed a genuine panic within me, concerned whether there would be enough for me by the time everyone else had helped themselves.

Later, I reflected on how I often feel that I am last in the queue for God's blessings. Is there really enough for me? I feel this way particularly in tough times while others appear content along life's way.

But then I looked at all those overflowing baskets of leftovers! There was more than enough. There was plenty for all. No one went hungry that day. Everyone was satisfied. I finally knew in my heart that God has more than enough to meet our deepest needs. God cherishes us and will nourish us. We all are invited to take and receive and to know God's love and care.

Prayer: *Thank you, God, that there is grace enough and love enough for each of us today and every day. Amen*

Thought for the day: God will meet all my needs (see Philippians 4:19).

Hilary Allen (England, United Kingdom)

PRAYER FOCUS: THOSE WITHOUT ENOUGH TO EAT   107

Learning about hope

Read Romans 5:1–5

Suffering produces endurance, and endurance produces character, and character produces hope.

Romans 5:3–4 (NRSV)

At the age of 40 I had a freak sporting accident that caused a near fatal stroke. It led to extensive damage to my health that would haunt me for many years. Basic abilities I had previously taken for granted – standing without help, walking without tripping, dressing without assistance, drinking without choking and speaking without slurring – were no longer natural. My senses of taste and smell were diminished.

Gradually, through prayer, support and hard work, I was able to rebuild my life. I found myself clinging to God more and more. Today's reading inspired me to keep on hoping. Slowly, I returned to my career as a professional counsellor and worked full time for another 25 years. A friend recently asked me what I learned about myself during recovery. I told him that I came to like the 'me' that emerged after the stroke. In my suffering, God taught me to nurture and maintain hope.

The apostle Paul, a man who knew suffering well, explains in today's quoted verse how suffering can lead to hope. I've experienced the truth that God can help us create something very good out of something very bad. When we face any difficult situation, the truth of God's presence with us enables us to have hope.

Prayer: *Dear God, help us to feel your presence with us in difficult times. Guide us as we seek to nurture and maintain hope in you. Amen*

Thought for the day: In my suffering, God can lead me to hope.

Ralph Thompson (Ohio, USA)

Completely calm

Read Matthew 8:23–27

Suddenly a furious storm came up on the lake, so that the waves swept over the boat. But Jesus was sleeping.
Matthew 8:24 (NIV)

The storm came out of nowhere. The water had been calm when they boarded the boat, but now the boat was rocking violently against the waves. They were terrified and quickly went over to the one who could help. But Jesus was sleeping. In a panic they woke him. 'Save us!' they shouted. 'We're going to drown!' As the waves were crashing, putting the boat and the disciples in peril, Jesus was napping, seemingly oblivious to it all.

In my life I sometimes feel like Jesus is taking a nap. Scared and over-whelmed, I don't see help coming any time soon. I want to scream for Jesus to wake up. 'Save me! I'm not going to make it this time!'

But down deep in my soul I know better. I know that a hundred other times I have called, and Jesus has been there – though sometimes later than I would have preferred.

In this story from Matthew's gospel, Jesus told the waves what to do, and they calmed completely. Jesus can do that in our lives too. Some-times, when there's no relief in sight, Jesus sends an answer. Sometimes it's by completely calming the circumstances; other times, it's by com-pletely calming us.

Prayer: *Dear Jesus, thank you for never leaving us in our time of need. Help us to fully trust you and your timing. Amen*

Thought for the day: Whatever I am going through, Jesus knows and cares about it.

Jen Chapman (West Virginia, USA)

God's way, not mine

Read Romans 12:9–21

Do not repay anyone evil for evil.
Romans 12:17 (NIV)

The atmosphere in my office was tense. My boss had scolded me, and I was hurt. Later, when I was alone, temptation overcame me as I brooded over his allegations, some of which were baseless. My anger got the better of me, and I shot off a scathing email to him.

I instantly regretted my deed. I had caused hurt and misunderstanding in my workplace. Later, this Bible verse came to mind: 'Do not repay anyone evil for evil.' Just because I had been hurt didn't justify my reaction. Scripture repeatedly urges us to forgive those who hurt us. In Romans 12, Paul wrote about blessing those who persecute us, even if it is our boss or a colleague. He wrote, 'Live at peace with everyone.'

Forgiveness is difficult. When we are hurt, it's hard to forget. Paul went on to write that we ought to 'overcome evil with good'. In order to do so we will need to humble ourselves before God and not take matters into our own hands. Surely our relationship with those at work and others in our lives will be stronger when we live in obedience to God's teaching from the apostle Paul.

Prayer: *O God, help us learn to forgive when we feel hurt by others, so that reconciliation may come. Amen*

Thought for the day: When I feel hurt, I can remember what scripture has taught me.

Sultana Butt (Karnataka, India)

Moving mountains

Read Matthew 17:14–20

'Truly I tell you, if you have faith the size of a mustard seed, you will say to this mountain, "Move from here to there", and it will move; and nothing will be impossible for you.'
Matthew 17:20 (NRSV)

When I moved from the city back to my small hometown and back to the little church where I had grown up, I assumed that the church was too small to be of much significance. 'Surely,' I thought, 'its light could not shine as bright as that of the large urban church I had attended in the city.' My assumptions were wrong.

Almost immediately, I learned that what the church lacked in numbers and resources was offset by the dedication of its members as they filled hundreds of buckets with cleaning supplies for flood victims and went out into the community to repair and maintain homes for residents. This little church moves mountains for the communities it helps and for the members who come together to serve.

People in Jesus' time thought of him in much the same way I once thought about my church. Most didn't think Jesus, born to poor parents from a small town, was the Messiah. He worked as a carpenter. He spent time with fishermen. How could a common man make any mark whatsoever on the world, much less be Saviour and Redeemer?

When we question the significance of our service, we can remember that the first disciples of Jesus were only twelve people. Though small in number, they revealed God's greatness to an entire world – and so can we.

Prayer: *Dear Father, no matter how small or insignificant we might feel, grant us the faith to serve others. Amen*

Thought for the day: I can accomplish great things through faith in Jesus Christ.

John Grube (Texas, USA)

PRAYER FOCUS: SMALL CONGREGATIONS

In the silence

Read 2 Timothy 1:5–10

May the God of peace… equip you with everything good for doing his will, and may he work in us what is pleasing to him.
Hebrews 13:20–21 (NIV)

'I'm sorry; there was nothing we could do,' the ER doctor said to the bereaved family. 'I'll leave you with the chaplain now.' The elderly woman and her son huddled together, weeping and glancing awkwardly at me. I panicked. Until then my shifts as a student chaplain had been routine. Uncomfortable and uncertain about how to proceed, I silently prayed for wisdom.

That night I discovered that I don't have to have the right words or experience or even age to join God in bringing comfort; I just have to be present and willing. God faithfully equipped me in that moment to help strangers in crisis.

Moving beyond our comfort zone forces us to rely on God to equip us for whatever confronts us. It might be serving at a homeless shelter, helping a single mother or elderly neighbour, or drawing near a stranger or friend in crisis. It can be uncomfortable, and we may feel tempted to withdraw in fear of saying or doing the wrong thing. But when we are willing simply to be present, we join with God, who is already at work. We leave the situation more connected to God and more connected to one another from our shared experience.

Prayer: *Dear God, strengthen us to be your loving presence to those who are hurting or in crisis. If we are led to speak, speak through us. Amen*

Thought for the day: Sometimes God speaks most powerfully through silence.

Sherry Graf (Colorado, USA)

Supporting hand

Read Psalm 139:1–12

If I take the wings of the morning and settle at the farthest limits of the sea, even there your hand shall lead me, and your right hand shall hold me fast.
Psalm 139:9–10 (NRSV)

In 2014 my family and I migrated from Pakistan to Canada. Although we had many comforts and blessings in Pakistan, some domestic situations led us to make the tough decision to move. I was quite concerned about settling and adjusting to a different part of the world. We prayed a lot about this concern.

Early in the morning on the day of our departure, as we were waiting at the airport terminal, I looked towards the wings of the plane we would board. Amid my mixed feelings, my thoughts moved to the above scripture verses. I felt with strong conviction that God's supporting hand would continue to be upon us. It was then that God's peace replaced my worries.

During the first few years, we faced many challenges and struggles. However God's guidance, provision, strength and support remained visible to us through our generous and supportive church friends. Ultimately my wife and I got good jobs in our professions, and our sons settled well into their studies.

Even in chaotic situations, as we keep on trusting God we can feel God's hand on us – leading, guiding, encouraging, providing for and protecting us.

Prayer: *Dear God, thank you for your guidance, strength and support no matter where we go. Amen*

Thought for the day: God's love and care for me has no borders.

Zafar Iqbal (Ontario, Canada)

Provided for

Read Luke 12:22–34

If you follow my statutes and keep my commandments and observe them faithfully, I will give you your rains in their season, and the land shall yield its produce.
Leviticus 26:3–4 (NRSV)

My husband grew up working in his family garden and still enjoys growing his own vegetables. One year, we had an abundance of heavy rain. Roads closed, bridges were washed out and large trees toppled over. When time to prepare the garden came, my husband was worried. The storms continued for days at a time. I often saw him stare at the puddles from the window and shake his head.

On a day it didn't rain, my husband walked to the edge of the plot to see if the sun had dried the soil enough to start tilling. From a distance he noticed small sprouts popping up from the ground. Since he hadn't planted anything, he strolled up for a closer look. He recognised the tiny vines immediately. Squash, cantaloupe, and watermelon from the previous year had reseeded and started to grow back.

As we gathered and ate our fresh harvest that year, Jesus' lesson in today's reading came to mind. For months my husband was concerned about starting his garden without realising that God was steps ahead. Just as our Lord reminded the disciples not to worry, my husband and I have learned to trust that God knows what we need and will always provide for us.

Prayer: *Dear Father in heaven, thank you for your constant love. Strengthen our faith so that we may grow closer to you. In Jesus' name. Amen*

Thought for the day: Relying on God opens me to new possibilities.

Kelly Desclos-Estes (Virginia, USA)

A son's wish to serve

Read Acts 20:32–35
'The Lord Jesus himself said: "It is more blessed to give than to receive."'
Acts 20:35 (NIV)

When my son began to have severe back pain seven years ago, nothing helped. After dealing with the pain for several years, he confided in me that the pain was becoming so debilitating that he would one day no longer be able to work in his job providing social services for teens. 'Dad,' he said through tears of pain, 'I want to serve in this world, not be served.'

A few months later, doctors discovered he had a massive tumour. He had stage 4 sarcoma. None of this, however, kept him from putting others first. He accepted his diagnosis and calmly asked his doctor how long he had to live. Four months later, as he was dying in the hospital, he consistently turned his focus on others. Whenever a nurse, doctor or visitor asked, 'How are you?' he always answered, 'I'm hanging in there. How are you?' I stood in awe of his courage and love for others.

In today's quoted verse, Paul shared Jesus' words with the early Christians: 'It is more blessed to give than to receive'. God calls us to serve one another, and my son did just that until the day he died. His last words were the Lord's Prayer we prayed together in his hospital room. His faithfulness has brought comfort and peace to my soul and has strengthened me in my faith.

Prayer: *Heavenly Father, help us to develop hearts that want to serve others as we follow you. Amen*

Thought for the day: How can I serve God today?

Steven Lee (Illinois, USA)

PRAYER FOCUS: SOMEONE WHO HAS LOST A CHILD TO CANCER

Always there

Read John 14:15–31

Jesus said to him, 'Have you believed because you have seen me? Blessed are those who have not seen and yet have come to believe.'
John 20:29 (NRSV)

I live in a two-storey house. When we do laundry, my mother irons our clothes downstairs and I have to climb steep stairs carrying piles of clothes with both hands. As I climb the stairs blindly with the clothes obstructing my view, I remember God. Because although I cannot see the step in front of me, I feel safe and supported knowing it is there.

My faith is very much like this at times. I believe even though I do not see God, and I pray because I know God is there. However, in the same way that I feel a certain fear of making a misstep on the stairs, there are moments when I have doubts about my faith and think, 'Can I trust God completely?' Sometimes my faith becomes weaker due to life challenges.

With care, we can reach the top of steep stairs, and we can look to God through prayer, Bible reading and the events of our lives for guidance. Although it is not easy to walk in faith, God knows this and helps us with infinite mercy.

Prayer: *Dear God, thank you for helping us when we are uncertain. Thank you for always being near when we pray. Amen*

Thought for the day: Prayer and Bible reading help me to feel God's presence.

Norma Sarian (São Paulo, Brazil)

Grabbing on to God

Read Mark 5:21–34

Even though I walk through the darkest valley, I will fear no evil, for you are with me; your rod and your staff, they comfort me.
Psalm 23:4 (NIV)

A short time after I had knee surgery, my wife had grab bars installed to help me get around our house. They were an incredible aid. Whenever I thought that my legs were going to give out, I could hold on to a grab bar.

Weak and tired knees aren't the only things that make us reach out for support. When life hands us one problem after another, we reach out for whatever help we can find. Perhaps it seems impious to speak of 'grabbing' on to God, but many of us have done that very thing. Often in times of distress, we don't meditate, we don't study the Bible, we don't pray anything more than 'Help!' We just grab on to the Holy One.

In today's reading, a woman touched Jesus' garment and received healing. But sometimes we don't want to merely touch Jesus' garment; we want to grab it with both hands! God, and our faith in God, is the ultimate support. Whether we deal with bad knees, financial woes, personal problems or the loss of a loved one, God can support us as nothing and no one else can. God offers the patience, wisdom, strength and insight – and sometimes sense of humour – that we need to deal with our problems. It is good to know that God is at hand to offer support that will last throughout our lives and beyond.

Prayer: *Thank you, Holy One, for always being near, our ever-present help in times of need. In Jesus' name we pray. Amen*

Thought for the day: No matter how I reach out, God is ready to support me.

Philip A. Rice (Michigan, USA)

PRAYER FOCUS: THOSE RECOVERING FROM SURGERY

My neighbours

Read Luke 10:25–37

'Which of these three do you think was a neighbour to the man who fell into the hands of robbers?' The expert in the law replied, 'The one who had mercy on him.' Jesus told him, 'Go and do likewise.'
Luke 10:36–37 (NIV)

I had called the helpline to fix a computer problem and was placed on hold. The music began to play while I was waiting. Not being a person who wastes time, I decided to read one of my devotionals for the day. The story was about a woman who realised her prayer life was focused too much on herself and her needs. She prayed to be able to broaden her prayer focus. While she was out for a walk, she began to pray for neighbours she did not know well and even strangers.

As I continued to wait, I took her idea and began to pray for the man who was helping me. I'm sure he often has to deal with people on the phone who are displeased and difficult to satisfy. I prayed he would come to know God if he didn't already. When our call concluded, I thanked him for his professionalism and wished him a good day. Even though I didn't know him personally, God considers him my neighbour. God desires to hear our concerns and prayers every day and wants to guide us, heal us and forgive us. Our prayers can extend beyond our family or community and include everyone in the whole world. They are all our neighbours.

Prayer: *Dear Lord, help us extend our prayers to people and situations we don't know well so that we can learn to embrace all people as our neighbours. Amen*

Thought for the day: Everyone I meet is my neighbour.

Lori Hulvey (Illinois, USA)

The best path

Read Psalm 25:1–6

Show me your ways, Lord, teach me your paths.
Psalm 25:4 (NIV)

One day, my colleague brought her four-year-old son, Jorge, to the office for a visit. After chatting with us for a bit, he was ready to leave. His mother was holding his hand firmly, but he was squirming to get free, trying to open the door to make his exit. He gave the impression that he knew which exit door to use and that he did not need his mother's guidance. I smiled and thought, 'How is it possible that this four-year-old is so independent and full of confidence?'

Later I reflected on how we, the children of God, often act the same way. Many times we exhibit Jorge's streak of independence and confidence. We firmly believe we know the best path to take, while God lovingly holds us by the hand to guide our steps. But we squirm to be free, wanting to move ahead on our own wisdom and strength. However, God knows the best path for us. We can discover God's paths through prayer, studying God's word in the Bible and consulting spiritual mentors.

God will not lead us astray. On that we can depend.

Prayer: *O God, we praise you for your presence with us. Help us to trust in your guidance for our lives. In the name of Jesus. Amen*

Thought for the day: My confidence rests in God, who leads me in right paths.

Jairon Otoniel Santana Suárez (Dominican Republic)

Waiting patiently

Read Psalm 130

Be still before the Lord and wait patiently for him.
Psalm 37:7 (NIV)

It was a normal sort of morning. I had put the dirty laundry in the washing machine and set it going, and I was just about to put my breakfast in the microwave when suddenly there was no power. I checked the circuit breakers, and found that the main switch was out, but nothing I did would reset it.

I phoned the emergency number that my landlord had supplied and asked for help. It took twelve hours for an electrician to reach me, and then it took him another two hours to find the problem. It turned out to be a badly wired junction box, where the insulation had melted. Had the circuit breakers not tripped, the house would have gone up in flames!

When things go wrong, I tend to over-react and become impatient for a resolution. In this case I had no choice but to wait patiently. And, as I discovered, the power cut also prevented something much worse happening.

So often when God calls us to wait, we can get impatient, but God always has a purpose for us, and we can learn from him in the waiting times.

Prayer: *Dear Lord, help us to use the waiting times of life to learn from you and grow in our walk with you.*

Thought for the day: I will be still before the Lord and wait patiently.

Hilary Hartley (England, United Kingdom)

Broken beauty

Read 2 Corinthians 12:1–10

I praise you because I am fearfully and wonderfully made; your works are wonderful, I know that full well.
Psalm 139:14 (NIV)

As I walked into the 800-year-old cathedral in Ireland, the stained-glass windows took my breath away. Everywhere I turned, there were stunning depictions of the life of Jesus. One window, near the front of the cathedral, caught my eye. It was of Jesus surrounded by people sitting at his feet to listen and learn from him. The closer I walked towards this magnificent piece of art, the more I became aware of the countless pieces of broken glass that made up each person who sat at the feet of Jesus.

Each figure was strikingly different. Yet each was looking for the same hope, peace and joy that comes from knowing Jesus as Saviour. At times we may feel like we have been broken into a million pieces – by the death of a loved one, by a devastating illness or by bad choices we have made. We can feel as if there is no hope of healing from this brokenness.

Jesus can take our broken pieces and, like those stained-glass windows, form beautiful works of art. As today's quoted verse reminds us, we are made by God. We can have faith that God can see the bigger picture and how each of us, as magnificent pieces of God's workmanship, can be used for God's glory.

Prayer: *Dear God, thank you for your limitless love and for meeting us in our brokenness. Continue to make us into beautiful works that bring glory to you. Amen*

Thought for the day: God can heal my brokenness and give me purpose.

Mendy Creswell Huskey (Tennessee, USA)

PRAYER FOCUS: ARTISANS

An important reminder

Read Lamentations 3:25–33

No one is cast off by the Lord forever… he will show compassion,
so great is his unfailing love.
Lamentations 3:31–32 (NIV)

It had rained throughout the night, and the morning felt gloomy and miserable to me. Dirt roads, black with mud, sloshed as I walked to work. My spirit was low.

Then I received news from my friend. My mum had died. She had been seriously ill for some time, but I had not expected her passing. I knew I should pray, but I could not muster a word of prayer. I was even unable to cry, but I was certain that the one who created the universe was with me.

Today what I miss most is something my mum said to me when I left for boarding school at age 12 and year after year. Each time I returned home, she would hug me and say, 'David, I hope you still go to church.' Each time I would answer that I could never forget church.

I was crushed as I worked through my mother's burial arrangements, and I laboured through an ensuing depression for three years. But though she was physically absent, the faith that she encouraged in me helped me through my devastation. Now, more than ten years later, whenever I read scripture, I find encouragement from God for the day's challenges.

Prayer: *Dear God, help us to remember that you will never abandon us, no matter the circumstances. Give us strength to persevere in our faith even as we mourn. Amen*

Thought for the day: Even in my grief, God is near.

David Angango (Nairobi, Kenya)

Loving God

Read Matthew 22:34–40

Whatever is true, whatever is noble, whatever is right, whatever is pure, whatever is lovely, whatever is admirable – if anything is excellent or praiseworthy – think about such things.
Philippians 4:8 (NIV)

In today's reading, Jesus said that the greatest commandment is to love the Lord with all our heart, all our soul and all our mind. Throughout my Christian walk, I learned to love God with all my heart and soul, but my mind had a mind of its own. Training my mind to love God became the answer to a huge problem I had with my thoughts.

Every morning I read scripture and pray to start my day. But by the time the day turns to evening, I have experienced many negative and unkind thoughts. The idea of loving God with all my mind has changed my thinking. I want to be more aware of my thoughts during the day and learn to replace them with healthier, more godly thoughts. For example, if I think an unkind thought about someone, I may follow the thought even further and eventually gossip about that person. Instead, I'm learning to confess the thought to God immediately and forgive myself. Then I think about what is admirable, excellent or praiseworthy. I want to love God with my mind, and over time I am learning to do that.

Prayer: *Dear Father, forgive us for our careless thoughts that do not honour you. Thank you for the scriptures that redirect our thoughts. Amen*

Thought for the day: Today I will turn my thoughts to God.

Nancy Brow (California, USA)

All things to all people

Read Matthew 18:1–5

I have become all things to all people, so I could save some by all possible means. All the things I do are for the sake of the gospel, so I can be a partner with it.
1 Corinthians 9:22–23 (CEB)

The teacher was preparing her class for my visit. 'Mrs Lewis is taking our assembly today. Does anyone remember Mrs Lewis?' A hand went up and the child answered, 'She is the little girl who tells us stories from the Bible.'

I laughed all day after that at the thought of still being regarded as a little girl. I had thought the years had long passed when I looked young for my age; I have now reached that time when I am making plans for a big 90th birthday, and I am very thankful for those who care for me as a 'dear little old lady'. So it is precious to find that this little girl recognised in me a child who loves Jesus and comes in faith to him. Didn't Jesus say that unless we become like little children, we will not enter his kingdom? And the apostle Paul said that he was willing to be made all things to all people.

Isn't that how God came to us? Jesus became human, born of a woman, just as we are. He became vulnerable, which meant he could be reviled and abused as well as worshipped. And most of all, he came so that you and I can call him Jesus, our Saviour.

Prayer: *Lord, may we accept every opportunity you give us to share the good news of Jesus and be willing to become all things to all people.*

Thought for the day: Whatever our circumstances, age or ability, God wants to use me to share his wonderful love.

Pauline Lewis (Wales, United Kingdom)

Life together

Read Hebrews 10:19–25

Let us consider how we may spur one another on towards love and good deeds, not giving up meeting together, as some are in the habit of doing, but encouraging one another – and all the more as you see the Day approaching.
Hebrews 10:24–25 (NIV)

None of us is perfect. I have tried to be a better person and to establish a better relationship with God by making a personal commitment to spending time alone, studying the Bible and worshiping God on my own. I have learned that I need some time alone with God, but that is not enough. I also need a community of faith where I can be in fellowship with others.

Sometimes God speaks to us through others, so we need fellowship and Communion. Since I began participating in my church choir and a young-adult group, I have learned a lot. I have improved myself in ways that would not be possible alone. Christian communities are precious gifts from God. We can encourage and build up one another in ways more amazing than we could ever imagine. God can speak to us through one another when we gather in love to work together in service to God.

Prayer: *Loving God, thank you for the gift of Christian community. Continue to reveal yourself to us as we fellowship with one another. We pray as Jesus taught us, 'Our Father in heaven, hallowed be your name, your kingdom come, your will be done, on earth as it is in heaven. Give us today our daily bread. And forgive us our debts, as we also have forgiven our debtors. And lead us not into temptation, but deliver us from the evil one.'* Amen*

Thought for the day: How does my Christian community strengthen my faith?

Mavula Sabbath Kefas (Baden-Württemberg, Germany)

Giving back

Read 2 Corinthians 9:6–15

Each of you should give what you have decided in your heart to give, not reluctantly or under compulsion, for God loves a cheerful giver.
2 Corinthians 9:7 (NIV)

One New Year's Eve when I was a young adult, I went to bed sobbing as I reflected on all that had gone wrong over the past year. I desperately prayed to God that the next year would be better.

A year later, I was back on my feet again. I felt overwhelmed by God's grace, and I wanted to do something to thank God.

At the time, I was not going to church consistently. I had just moved into a new area and was still trying to choose a church. I am also visually impaired and can't drive, so I had to ask others for rides.

I had not tithed since I started living on my own. So I added up my assets and gross income and sent a check worth 10 percent of the total to a local church, even though I wasn't a member. I also sent a note that read, 'Use this to God's glory.'

I didn't want to be thanked. It was my way of giving back to God a portion of all that God had given me. It doesn't seem like much considering the blessings God pours out in abundance.

Prayer: *Gracious God, thank you for all the blessings you have given us. May our gifts reflect our gratitude for all that you have done. Amen*

Thought for the day: What will I give back to God today?

Christine Adhikari (Georgia, USA)

Only trying to help

Read Romans 8:28–39

If God is for us, who can be against us? He who did not spare his own Son, but gave him up for us all – how will he not also, along with him, graciously give us all things?
Romans 8:31–32 (NIV)

On a recent stay at my sister-in-law's house, I noticed a baby robin that had fallen into a basement window well. The well was too deep for the bird to free itself, and I soon realised that I would have to rescue it. I moved quickly to scoop the bird from the window well. But when I stooped down beside it, it began to chirp wildly in fear. Soon, I was bombarded by the baby robin's family, who had been watching from a nearby tree.

After rescuing the robin, I realised that the small bird had perceived my best intentions as a desire to harm it. Perhaps if the robin had known I was trying to help, it would not have so vehemently resisted.

Sometimes, we are like that baby bird. We find ourselves in some predicament, often of our own making, but we don't recognise God's power to rescue us.

May our faith remind us that God is for us, not against us, and that God cares for us far more deeply than we can imagine. When we cry out to God in prayer, God can rescue us from our deepest fear and despair.

Prayer: *Heavenly Father, thank you for loving and caring for us. Forgive us when we resist your help. In Jesus' name we pray. Amen*

Thought for the day: God is for me, not against me.

Chuck Kralik (Missouri, USA)

God still loves us

Read John 11:1–16

Though Jesus loved Martha and her sister and Lazarus, after having heard that Lazarus was ill, he stayed two days longer in the place where he was.

John 11:5–6 (NRSV)

Martha and Mary were dealing with a painful experience: their brother was ill, and they needed help. When they sent for Jesus, they must have hoped that he would come to them immediately, but he did not come for two more days.

Martha and Mary felt they needed an immediate response, because their brother was deathly ill. But Jesus responded to their request in his timing, waiting two more days. During that time Lazarus died. We may wonder, as the sisters must have, if Jesus really loved them, why would he not set aside whatever he was doing and help them?

We often pray expecting immediate answers, but we don't always receive them. In those times, we may ask, 'Where are you, Lord? If you love me, why am I still in this situation?' But when we don't get immediate answers to our prayers, it does not mean that God does not love us. Though God may not come to our aid immediately, God is mindful of us and will come in time. And in God's timing, God's love will shine through to us.

Prayer: *Dear Lord, help us to remember that you love us always, even when things don't go the way we hope. Amen*

Thought for the day: Even when my prayers seem unanswered, God still loves me.

Enid Adah Nyinomujuni (Dar es Salaam, Tanzania,

God-given gifts

Read 1 Corinthians 12:4–11

You created my inmost being; you knit me together in my mother's womb… Your eyes saw my unformed body; all the days ordained for me were written in your book before one of them came to be.
Psalm 139:13, 16 (NIV)

'I have my own church!' I shouted when I called to tell my parents that I had received an opportunity to play piano for a church full-time. It was something I had not thought possible.

My mother began teaching me how to play the piano at a young age. As a child, I played in many recitals; but after high school, I stopped playing. It wasn't until I joined the church I am a member of now that I began playing again. Time stood still as I played. One day, someone heard me playing and asked if I would play a song during the worship service. I agreed. After the service, several people thanked me for playing and for sharing my talent. My talent?

When I read the scriptures for today, I am reminded that before we are fully formed, God knows our talents. Our God-given gifts are meant to be used to serve one another and to glorify God. Through the gift of music, I am able to praise God and share my faith with others. Thanks be to God for our gifts!

Prayer: *Heavenly Father, help us to recognise our gifts and talents so that we may use them to serve one another and glorify your name. Amen*

Thought for the day: How can I use my gift to glorify God today?

Janet Pierce (Tennessee, USA)

The perfect cross

Read John 19:17–30

'Whoever wants to be my disciple must deny themselves and take up their cross daily and follow me.'
Luke 9:23 (NIV)

Sitting in prison, I have learned to occupy my time with things I normally would not do, such as creative writing and drawing. With my new-found Christian walk, I decided to draw a cross as a visual reminder of what Jesus did for me. I am a bit of a perfectionist, and since the prison allows only a pen (no pencils) and paper, the task was more difficult than I expected. Rulers are not allowed either, so using the notepad for a straightedge made it hard to measure the lines for exact length and width. I also tried to use proper shading to make the wood appear to have age rings and knots, as if it had come from the lumberyard.

But as I struggled to draw the perfect cross, I realised that the cross Jesus carried probably wasn't perfect. It might have been weathered, with splits and edges that weren't perfectly straight. After hours of drawing, trying to get all the details perfect, I realised there were only two things perfect about Jesus' cross – Jesus himself and the fact that he died for the sins of us all. Thanks to Jesus' willingness to die, God has forgiven my imperfections. Every day, I can carry my cross in service to God, accepting God's love and grace.

Prayer: *Dear God, thank you for loving us, especially when we do not feel lovable. Thank you for your forgiveness and grace. In Jesus' name we pray. Amen*

Thought for the day: God loves me more than I could ever imagine.

Steven Paul Simmons (Texas, USA)

Redemption

Read Psalm 31:19–24
Praise be to the Lord, for he showed me the wonders of his love.
Psalm 31:21 (NIV)

It happened in Soviet Ukraine in 1978. I worked in the glass factory and lived in the workers' dormitory. One day I was injured at work and was recovering in my room. Suddenly the door was thrown open, and I was surrounded by militia officers. They started asking questions about my next-door neighbour, Nikolaj. It turned out that he had distributed anti-Soviet leaflets and then committed suicide in front of the railway station.

Nikolaj was a quiet and friendly man, and the news shocked me deeply. His death led me to think about the meaning of my life, and after a while I sank into a spiritual crisis. Knowing my anguish, God sent to our factory a young man who shared openly his faith in Christ. He helped me to find a church, where I decided to become a follower of Jesus.

That experience happened many years ago. Now I am happily married, and our children have found the same faith in Christ. I still remember my good neighbour, Nikolaj, who could not see any hope for his life in this world. And I still remember the young man who shared his faith with me and offered hope that changed my life. Through the grace of God, let's commit our lives to offering that same hope to our friends and neighbours.

Prayer: *Dear God, lead us into your light, love and eternal life. Amen*

Thought for the day: I can be a reminder of God's grace for others.

Serhiy Lohinov (Ukraine)

PRAYER FOCUS: SOMEONE WHO NEEDS MY SUPPORT

Nature's healing

Read Job 12:7–10

Light is sweet, and it pleases the eyes to see the sun.
Ecclesiastes 11:7 (NIV)

A while ago, I suffered quite a few losses in a short period of time. Days were filled with sadness as sorrow after sorrow came my way. Every day seemed gray.

I would spend time in the early morning just outside my back door. I don't know what led me there, but I suspect that it was God's loving provision. At the earliest hint of light, I went to the patio and breathed in nature. For an hour or more, I let God's creation soothe my melancholy.

As the sun crept slowly through the huge river birch, sometimes a breeze stirred the leaves. Always, the birds sang. The call of the Eurasian collared doves sounded like 'Praise Je-sus! Praise Je-sus!' Some days the sky was blue and clear or had puffy white clouds floating about. Other days, the sky was streaked with orange and pink. Whatever the design of the day, it was beautiful and calming. The wonder of God's creation lifted my sadness and helped me through.

God cares when we hurt and sometimes provides healing in unexpected ways. As we keep ourselves open with expectation, God will give us the perfect balm for our sorrow. It could even be something like the early morning sky that has been there for us all along.

Prayer: *Creator God, thank you for the wonder of your creation through which you mend our hurting hearts. Amen*

Thought for the day: When I am hurting, God offers healing in unexpected ways.

Pat Luffman Rowland (Tennessee, USA)

Small group questions

Wednesday 5 May

1 Describe a time when you have seen someone coming to Christ after spending time around Christian examples. How did you see God working in the situation? What did you learn from it?

2 How do you express your faith to others? In what ways do you share Jesus' love if you are not specifically talking about it?

3 Have you ever felt discouraged when someone didn't believe in Jesus after you witnessed to them? How did you respond? What helps you to remain patient in times like this?

4 How does your church encourage you to share your faith with others? Whose example has been most helpful to you as you prepare to share your faith? What situations make you hesitant or uncomfortable sharing your faith?

5 Besides Damaris and Dionysius, what other biblical figures come to mind when you read today's meditation about sharing Christ's love? Why? What can we learn from their stories?

Wednesday 12 May

1 How do you feel when someone you haven't spoken to in a while gets in touch with you? When do you try to contact someone you haven't spoken to in a while? In what ways can you use your interactions with others to share God's love?

2 When you experience God communicating with you, is it dramatic, like Isaiah's experience, or is it more subtle, like today's writer describes? What has God communicated to you recently?

3 How do you make time to listen for God's still small voice? How is your day changed when you take time to listen to God's voice?

4 When you are unsure of what God is guiding you to do, what spiritual practices help you find clarity? What scripture passages help you?

5   In what ways does your faith community encourage you to listen to God? How has your faith community helped you to act on God's guidance?

Wednesday 19 May

1   What are some of your most treasured books, stories or poems from childhood? How were you introduced to them? Why are they important to you?

2   What scripture passage has held meaning for you over a long period of time? How has your understanding of it changed over time?

3   Name some ways scripture has been a gift in your life. How does scripture draw you closer to God? What brings you back to scripture when you haven't read the Bible in a while?

4   Which scripture passages would you like to spend more time studying? What practices will you use to help you unfold the words as the psalmist suggests?

5   Who or what helps you to find meaning and beauty in God's words? How does your church help you find meaning in scripture?

Wednesday 26 May

1   Have you ever disagreed with someone so strongly that you would consider them an 'enemy'? Did you want peace or vindication? How did the situation resolve?

2   When have you felt satisfied by an outcome but you were not at peace about it? What role does your faith play in finding both satisfaction and peace in life?

3   Do you find it hard to pray for those whom you disagree with? What scripture verses or spiritual practices help you? If it is not difficult for you, why do you find it easy to pray for those you disagree with?

4   When have you observed that your prayers for others brought a change in you? How do you think prayer can transform us?

5 How do you find unity with other Christians? Who in your life serves as an example of loving others? How do you strive to show mercy and love to everyone around you?

Wednesday 2 June

1 Describe a time when having someone listen compassionately made a difference for you. What did this experience teach you about how to listen to others?

2 How can you tell when someone needs your attention and compassion? How do you respond? Is it easy or difficult for you to share God's mercy and love in these situations?

3 Do you feel sympathetic towards those who are incarcerated? Why or why not? What prayers and other spiritual practices could make you more sympathetic?

4 What scripture passages encourage you when you feel isolated? What biblical figures remind you of the importance of being sympathetic to the struggles of other people? How do you apply what you learn from these stories to your life?

5 Do you feel called to participate in a pen pal or other prison ministry programme? In what other ways could you minister to those who are incarcerated? In what ways could you minster to people who are figuratively imprisoned?

Wednesday 9 June

1 How has the Covid-19 pandemic affected you and those you love? How have you responded to your feelings of anxiety? Where have you found the most peace and joy?

2 Today's writer was encouraged by her friend's example of praying and reading scripture. Who encourages you in your faith? In what ways do they encourage you?

3 When you experience anxiety over the unknown, what are your prayers like? How are your prayers during such times different than when you feel more secure?

4 Which scripture verses bring you the most comfort during anxious times? Why? Which Bible stories best remind you of God's presence in our lives?

5 How can you support someone experiencing anxiety or fear? If you are feeling anxious or fearing the unknown right now, how can you lean on God and on others in your faith community?

Wednesday 16 June

1 If you see a need in your community, are you eager to fill it or do you hope someone else will? Why?

2 When you are afraid to risk failing at something, what do you do? How do you trust in God's help when you try to do something that scares you?

3 Describe a time when God has magnified something small to fit a need in your life. How did that experience give you hope?

4 What spiritual practices give you courage to risk failing? What scripture passages remind you that anything is possible with God?

5 What needs do you see in your church today? What needs do you see in your community? How can you help fill those needs?

Wednesday 23 June

1 Do you remember what it was like to be a child and to see the world as a child does? What do you think it means to have faith like a child?

2 Today's writer says that the children in his class pray for the needs of others and trust that God is listening. Why do you think this is so? What can we learn from these children?

3 What distracts you when you pray? Do you worry about saying the right things, about daily stresses or about more 'urgent' needs? What helps you regain focus when you pray so that you can have a real encounter with God?

4 Besides expressing prayers honestly and trustingly, what can you learn from the children around you? How can you implement those lessons in your faith and in your life?

5 Who and what is on your prayer list today? What Bible verses strengthen your trust that God will hear your prayer?

Wednesday 30 June

1 Recall a time when your life was undergoing a major change. How did you feel during that time? What role did your faith play in how you responded to the change?

2 When you are facing a time of crisis, what scripture passages bring you the most comfort? Do you repeat them like today's writer, or do you interact with the verses in another way? Explain how you use scripture during such times.

3 In what ways does memorising Bible verses help you? How do you go about memorising a new scripture? What verse would you like to memorise next? Why?

4 What do the 'I am' and 'I will' statements from Isaiah mean to you? How do they bring you peace?

5 In times of crisis, what spiritual practices, prayers, activities or people comfort you the most? How can you share God's comfort with others who are going through a crisis?

Wednesday 7 July

1 If you commute, how do you use that time? If you do not commute, what part of your daily routine would allow you to spend time in worship?

2 When have you found a community of worship in an unexpected place? How did you find that community? How did it enrich your life?

3 Have you ever had the opportunity to worship alongside someone who holds beliefs unlike your own? If so, what was that experience like? What can we learn from worshipping alongside people who hold beliefs different from our own?

4   How do you strive to be a witness of Christ's love to the world? How do your actions invite others to worship?

5   What do you find beautiful about interfaith community? What do you find difficult about it? In what ways would you like to see more diversity in your faith community? How might you take steps towards that end?

Wednesday 14 July

1   Have you ever lived far from family, only seeing them occasionally? If so, what did you learn about family and connection from that circumstance? If not, what has being near your relatives taught you about about family and connection?

2   Recall the 'worst' present you ever received. What was it? When have you received a present that you only began to appreciate over time?

3   When you tire of praying for a certain person or situation, what scripture passages encourage you to persist? What spiritual practices help you to remain hopeful when you feel like your prayers aren't doing any good?

4   Today's writer changed his perspective on the bookmark after learning more about his grandmother's faith. Why does gaining deeper understanding often change our perspective? What biblical characters serve as examples of this for you?

5   When you pray for others, do you often see results right away? How do you remain patient in prayer? How are you and your faith affected when you pray for others?

Wednesday 21 July

1   Recall a time when missing only a small amount of something made a big difference. What can that situation teach you about both community and faith?

2   What scripture passages remind you of the importance of 'adding' to those around you? In what ways do these passages help you? How do you apply them to your daily life?

3 What does it mean to you to be salt? How do you strive to be salt each day? In what ways do you find assurance that you are being salt to others?

4 When has someone used their faith to help bring out the best in you? What was your response? How did the experience change you? How can you strive to use your faith to help others in similar ways?

5 Name some ways you can join together with your siblings in faith to transform the flavour of life around the world,

Wednesday 28 July

1 When you read the story of Lot's wife, what do you think about her decision to look back? Do you understand why she might have done so? What do you think you would have done had you been in her place?

2 Recall a time when you struggled to move forward because you weren't able to grieve what you were leaving behind. What did you do to help yourself move forward? What role did your faith play in the situation?

3 What consequences have you experienced when you couldn't let go of the past and move forward? How does God comfort you in such times?

4 What scripture verses encourage you to have confidence in God's path for you? What verses remind you most of God's desire for our good? How do these verses equip us to deal with change?

5 Who in your life helps you keep your eyes focused on God's will for you? How does your faith community support you when you are trying to let go of something? How can you encourage others who are working to move forward?

Wednesday 4 August

1 Who has been a spiritual mentor for you? Name the most memorable lesson that they taught you. How has that lesson served you in your faith journey?

2 What do you think makes the prayer in today's meditation a 'big little prayer'? What is your big little prayer? When do you pray it? How does it help you?

3 Do you ever feel the need to pray long prayers or to say certain things in your prayers? Why or why not? Is there a time and place for different kinds of prayer? Do certain prayers help you more than others? Explain.

4 What scripture passages remind you of the importance of prayer and trusting God? Which biblical prayers stand out to you as examples of faithful prayer? What can you learn from them and apply to your prayer life?

5 What seeds of faith have you sowed recently? Name ways you have been intentional about sharing your faith with others. What role does prayer play when you are sharing your faith with others?

Wednesday 11 August

1 When have you needed to comfort someone but felt unsure of how to do so? How did you handle the situation? What was the outcome? What did you learn?

2 When you see someone in crisis, what is your response? Do you feel an instinct to shy away? How do you draw near and remain present with them? In what ways do you offer them God's love and comfort? In what ways is your response different depending on how well you know the person?

3 Are you encouraged to know that you can join God in bringing comfort to others, without having certain words or acting a certain way? How have you found this to be true in your life? Where in scripture do we see examples of this?

4 Do you agree that God often speaks most powerfully through silence? How do you hear God in silence? In what ways do you hear God speaking through others? How do you hope God speaks through you?

5 When do you feel most connected to God? When do you feel most connected to others? What shared experiences draw you closer to other people? What draws you closer to people outside your immediate community?

Wednesday 18 August

1 Recall a time when you felt that you knew the right thing to do and tried to force your way. Did you get your way? Was the outcome what you hoped for? What did you learn?

2 Do you think it is good to be independent and confident? Do you feel that you can be too independent and confident? How do you know when to be independent and confident and when to ask God for guidance? Are these mutually exclusive?

3 Does God's loving guidance ever frustrate you? How do you react when God guides you in a direction you were not hoping to go? What prayers, Bible passages or spiritual practices help you to accept God's direction in your life?

4 Who in your life helps you to remember God's presence and to follow God's paths? Name some biblical characters who are good examples of following God's guidance. In what ways do you strive to help others who may be struggling to accept God's guidance?

5 How does your church discern and follow God's guidance? How does your church community encourage you to follow God's guidance? In what ways could it be more encouraging?

Wednesday 25 August

1 When you are going through difficult times, what are your prayers like? When you cry out to God, how does God respond?

2 What obstacles do you face when trying to find Christian community? How do you overcome those obstacles to find community? In what ways is your faith enriched by fellowship with other Christians?

3 Do you find tithing difficult? Do you think that it is important that we tithe? Why or why not? Are there ways to tithe other than giving money? Explain.

4 How do you give back to God? In what ways do you express your gratitude for God's blessings and grace? What Bible passages remind you of the importance of giving back to God joyfully and willingly?

5 To whom can you extend God's love and grace today? How can you give to others from what God has given you? In what ways can you better use your blessings to God's glory?

Journal page

Journal page

Journal page

Journal page

Become a Friend of BRF
and give regularly
to support our ministry

We help people of all ages to grow in faith

We encourage and support individual Christians and churches as they serve and resource the changing spiritual needs of communities today.

Through **Anna Chaplaincy**
we're enabling churches to provide
spiritual care to older people

Through **Living Faith**
we're nurturing faith and resourcing
life-long discipleship

Through **Messy Church**
we're helping churches to reach out
to families

Through **Parenting for Faith**
we're supporting parents as they raise
their children in the Christian faith

Our ministry is only possible because of the generous support of individuals, churches, trusts and gifts in wills.

As we look to the future and make plans, **regular donations make a huge difference** in ensuring we can both start and finish projects well.

By becoming a Friend of BRF and giving regularly to our ministry you are partnering with us in the gospel and helping change lives.

How your gift makes a difference

£2 a month — Helps us to develop **Living Faith** resources to use in care homes and communities

£10 a month — Helps us to support churches running the **Parenting for Faith** course and stand alongside parents

£5 a month — Helps us to support **Messy Church** volunteers and resource and grow the wider network

£20 a month — Helps us to resource **Anna Chaplaincy** and improve spiritual care for older people

 ## How to become a Friend of BRF

Set up a Direct Debit donation at **brf.org.uk/donate** or find out how to set up a Standing Order at **brf.org.uk/friends**

Contact the fundraising team

Email: giving@brf.org.uk
Tel: +44 (0)1235 462305
Post: Fundraising team, BRF, 15 The Chambers, Vineyard, Abingdon OX14 3FE

Good to know

If you have any questions, or if you want to change your regular donation or stop giving in the future, do get in touch.

Registered with

FR

FUNDRAISING REGULATOR

SHARING OUR VISION – MAKING A ONE-OFF GIFT

I would like to make a donation to support BRF.
Please use my gift for:

☐ Where it is most needed ☐ Anna Chaplaincy ☐ Living Faith
☐ Messy Church ☐ Parenting for Faith

Title	First name/initials	Surname
Address		
		Postcode
Email		
Telephone		
Signature		Date

Our ministry is only possible because of the generous support of individuals, churches, trusts and gifts in wills.

giftaid it You can add an extra 25p to every £1 you give.

Please treat as Gift Aid donations all qualifying gifts of money made

☐ today, ☐ in the past four years, ☐ and in the future.

I am a UK taxpayer and understand that if I pay less Income Tax and/or Capital Gains Tax in the current tax year than the amount of Gift Aid claimed on all my donations, it is my responsibility to pay any difference.

☐ My donation does not qualify for Gift Aid.

Please notify BRF if you want to cancel this Gift Aid declaration, change your name or home address, or no longer pay sufficient tax on your income and/or capital gains.

Please complete other side of form ➲

SHARING OUR VISION – MAKING A ONE-OFF GIFT

Please accept my gift of:

☐ £2 ☐ £5 ☐ £10 ☐ £20 Other £ ☐

by (*delete as appropriate*):

☐ Cheque/Charity Voucher payable to 'BRF'

☐ MasterCard/Visa/Debit card/Charity card

Name on card

Card no. ☐☐☐☐ ☐☐☐☐ ☐☐☐☐ ☐☐☐☐

Expires end ☐M☐M ☐Y☐Y Security code* ☐☐☐

*Last 3 digits on the reverse of the card
ESSENTIAL IN ORDER TO PROCESS
YOUR PAYMENT

Signature   Date

☐ I would like to leave a gift to BRF in my will.
Please send me further information.

For help or advice regarding making a gift, please contact
our fundraising team +44 (0)1865 462305

Your privacy

We will use your personal data to process this transaction.
From time to time we may send you information about the
work of BRF that we think may be of interest to you. Our
privacy policy is available at **brf.org.uk/privacy**. Please
contact us if you wish to discuss your mailing preferences.

Registered with

FUNDRAISING
REGULATOR

 Please complete other side of form

Please return this form to 'Freepost BRF'
No other address information or stamp is needed

The Bible Reading Fellowship is a Registered Charity (233280)

UR0221

The 'liminal seasons of life' – those transition times in which we have left one season of stability but not yet arrived at the next – can be times of great disorientation. Yet, for good or for ill, they are also the most transformative. In *The Space Between*, Mark Bradford provides the reader with a biblical and theological understanding of such seasons of life, connects them with the resources to live faithfully through them, and offers strength and hope for the journey.

The Space Between
The disruptive seasons we want to hide from, and why we need them
Mark Bradford
978 0 85746 825 3 £9.99
brfonline.org.uk

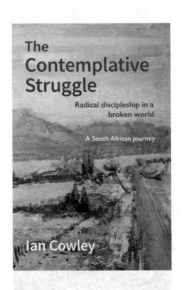

How do we embrace and work out our call to be disciples in a broken world? In *The Contemplative Struggle*, Ian Cowley sets the central themes of the gospel of John alongside each other – abiding in Christ, conflict, light and darkness, obedience, loving one another – and explores how these can be reconciled in daily life. Drawing on his experience of living in his native South Africa during the apartheid era and challenging understandings of contemplative prayer and spirituality as essentially inward discipline, he highlights the urgent need for Christians to be active in transforming a suffering world and paints a compelling picture of radical discipleship for today.

The Contemplative Struggle
Radical discipleship in a broken world
Ian Cowley
978 0 85746 982 3 £8.99
brfonline.org.uk

How to encourage Bible reading in your church

BRF has been helping individuals connect with the Bible for over 90 years. We want to support churches as they seek to encourage church members into regular Bible reading.

Order a Bible reading resources pack

This pack is designed to give your church the tools to publicise our Bible reading notes. It includes:

- Sample Bible reading notes for your congregation to try.
- Publicity resources, including a poster.
- A church magazine feature about Bible reading notes.

The pack is free, but we welcome a £5 donation to cover the cost of postage. If you require a pack to be sent outside the UK or require a specific number of sample Bible reading notes, please contact us for postage costs. More information about what the current pack contains is available on our website.

How to order and find out more

- Visit **biblereadingnotes.org.uk/for-churches**.
- Telephone BRF on +44 (0)1865 319700 Mon–Fri 9.30–17.00.
- Write to us at BRF, 15 The Chambers, Vineyard, Abingdon OX14 3FE.

Keep informed about our latest initiatives

We are continuing to develop resources to help churches encourage people into regular Bible reading, wherever they are on their journey. Join our email list at **brfonline.org.uk/signup** to stay informed about the latest initiatives that your church could benefit from.

Subscriptions

The Upper Room is published in January, May and September.

Individual subscriptions

The subscription rate for orders for 4 or fewer copies includes postage and packing:

The Upper Room annual individual subscription   £18.00

Group subscriptions

Orders for 5 copies or more, sent to ONE address, are post free:
The Upper Room annual group subscription   £14.25

Please do not send payment with order for a group subscription. We will send an invoice with your first order.

Please note that the annual billing period for group subscriptions runs from 1 May to 30 April.

Copies of the notes may also be obtained from Christian bookshops.

Single copies of *The Upper Room* cost £4.75.

Prices valid until 30 April 2022.

Giant print version

The Upper Room is available in giant print for the visually impaired, from:

Torch Trust for the Blind
Torch House
Torch Way
Northampton Road
Market Harborough
LE16 9HL

Tel: +44 (0)1858 438260
torchtrust.org

THE UPPER ROOM: INDIVIDUAL/GIFT SUBSCRIPTION FORM

All our Bible reading notes can be ordered online by visiting brfonline.org.uk/subscriptions

❑ I would like to take out a subscription myself (complete your name and address details once)

❑ I would like to give a gift subscription (please provide both names and addresses)

Title .... First name/initials .... Surname ....

Address ....

.... Postcode ....

Telephone .... Email ....

Gift subscription name ....

Gift subscription address ....

.... Postcode ....

Gift message (20 words max. or include your own gift card):

....

....

Please send *The Upper Room* beginning with the September 2021 / January 2022 / May 2022 issue (*delete as appropriate*):

Annual individual subscription ❑ £18.00

Optional donation* to support the work of BRF £ ....

Total enclosed £ .... (cheques should be made payable to 'BRF')

*Please complete and return the Gift Aid declaration on page 159 to make your donation even more valuable to us.

Method of payment

❑ Cheque (made payable to BRF) ❑ MasterCard / Visa

Card no. ☐☐☐☐ ☐☐☐☐ ☐☐☐☐ ☐☐☐☐

Expires end ☐☐ ☐☐ Security code* ☐☐☐ Last 3 digits on the reverse of the card

*ESSENTIAL IN ORDER TO PROCESS THE PAYMENT

THE UPPER ROOM: GROUP SUBSCRIPTION FORM

> **All our Bible reading notes can be ordered online by visiting brfonline.org.uk/subscriptions**

☐ Please send me .... copies of *The Upper Room* September 2021 / January 2022 / May 2022 issue (*delete as appropriate*)

Title .... First name/initials .... Surname ....

Address ....

.... Postcode ....

Telephone .... Email ....

Please do not send payment with this order. We will send an invoice with your first order.

Christian bookshops: All good Christian bookshops stock BRF publications. For your nearest stockist, please contact BRF.

Telephone: The BRF office is open Mon–Fri 9.30–17.00. To place your order, telephone +44 (0)1865 319700.

Online: brfonline.org.uk/group-subscriptions

☐ Please send me a Bible reading resources pack to encourage Bible reading in my church

Please return this form with the appropriate payment to:
BRF, 15 The Chambers, Vineyard, Abingdon OX14 3FE
To read our terms and find out about cancelling your order, please visit **brfonline.org.uk/terms**.

The Bible Reading Fellowship is a Registered Charity (233280

UR0221

order

Delivery times within the UK are normally 15 working days. Prices are correct at the time of going to press but may change without prior notice.

le	Price	Qty	Total
e Space Between	£9.99		
e Contemplative Struggle	£8.99		

POSTAGE AND PACKING CHARGES			
er value	UK	Europe	Rest of world
er £7.00	£2.00		
0–£29.99	£3.00	Available on request	Available on request
00 and over	FREE		

Total value of books	
Postage and packing	
Donation*	
Total for this order	

* Please complete the Gift Aid declaration below

se complete in BLOCK CAPITALS

tle .... First name/initials .... Surname...

ddress..

.... Postcode ....

c. No. .... Telephone ....

nail...

e Bible Reading Fellowship Gift Aid Declaration

giftaid it

ase treat as Gift Aid donations all qualifying gifts of money made

☐ today, ☐ in the past four years, ☐ and in the future **or** ☐ My donation does not qualify for Gift Aid.

m a UK taxpayer and understand that if I pay less Income Tax and/or Capital Gains Tax in the rrent tax year than the amount of Gift Aid claimed on all my donations, it is my responsibility bay any difference.

ase notify BRF if you want to cancel this declaration, change your name or home address, no longer pay sufficient tax on your income and/or capital gains.

ethod of payment

☐ Cheque (made payable to BRF) ☐ MasterCard / Visa

rd no. ☐☐☐☐ ☐☐☐☐ ☐☐☐☐ ☐☐☐☐ ☐☐☐☐ ☐☐☐☐

bires end ☐M☐M ☐Y☐Y Security code* ☐☐☐ Last 3 digits on the reverse of the card

nature* .... Date .... /............ /............

SENTIAL IN ORDER TO PROCESS THE PAYMENT

se return this form to: BRF, 15 The Chambers, Vineyard, Abingdon OX14 3FE | enquiries@brf.org.uk

ad our terms and find out about cancelling your order, please visit **brfonline.org.uk/terms**.

The Bible Reading Fellowship (BRF) is a Registered Charity (233280)

Enabling all ages to grow in faith

Anna Chaplaincy
Living Faith
Messy Church
Parenting for Faith

The Bible Reading Fellowship (BRF) is a Christian charity that resources individuals and churches. Our vision is to enable people of all ages to grow in faith and understanding of the Bible and to see more people equipped to exercise their gifts in leadership and ministry.

To find out more about our ministries, visit
brf.org.uk